INSIDE

KT-555-312

LittleBrother
B O O K S

Published 2021.
Little Brother Books, Ground Floor, 23 Southernhay East, Exeter, Devon, EX1 1QL
Printed in Poland. ul. Połczynska 99,01-303 Warszawa
books@littlebrotherbooks.co.uk | www.littlebrotherbooks.co.uk

The Little Brother Books trademarks, logos, email and website addresses and the GamesWarrior logo and imprint are sole and exclusive properties of Little Brother Books Limited.

This is an unofficial and independently written book, the inclusion of any logos, images, quotes and references does not imply endorsement. Whilst every care has been taken in researching and writing this book, due to the nature of the subject matter, some information may change over time.

Fortnite is a registered trademark of Epic Games. The screenshots and artwork shown in this guide were taken from Fortnite in game screenshots, a game created and published by Epic Games. This is a 100% unofficial and independent guide, which is in no way licensed, authorised or endorsed by or otherwise connected in anyway with Epic Games or any other individuals from Epic Games and authors of Fortnite. All copyrights and trademarks are recognised and used specifically for the purpose of criticism, review and reportage.

Images used under license from Shutterstock.com

A BRIEF HISTORY OF
FORTNITE

CHAPTER 1

The many seasons of Chapter 1 revealed an ongoing battle for control of the Zero Point, a glowing blue orb that was home to an immense amount of power. No-one knows exactly what gives the Zero Point its power, or even exactly what it can do, but one thing did become clear: it enabled characters to travel between different dimensions and even different times. Many speculated that the Zero Point was being used by The Unknown Order – a mysterious group about whom little is known – to keep the Fortnite island in an infinite loop, helped by Agent Jonesy in doing so.

At the end of Chapter 1, it seemed as though the power of the Zero Point had proven too much for even the Order to contain, as the island was sucked into a giant black hole after The Scientist – a member of The Seven, sworn enemies of The Unknown Order – had built a rocket to escape the island.

CHAPTER 2 SEASON 1

After two days without Fortnite, gamers all over the world finally woke up to find their favourite game was back online again. What they found when they logged back in was the single most spectacular change in Fortnite's history to that point – and to date, the biggest set of changes we have ever witnessed.

The Zero Point had vanished, and with it, the old island – completely. In its place was a totally new island that was home to two warring political factions – Alter and Ego – who were desperately battling each other to take control of the island.

Fortnite's new home was a rather barren and empty affair, larger than before and home to greater distances between named locations. The weaponry on offer was also pretty stark, with all the more complex weapons seemingly disappearing with the Zero Point and leaving simple weapons like shotguns and assault rifles behind instead.

All the cars had disappeared too, but in their place were motorboats, which enabled players to navigate the new islands system of waterways and rivers. Those rivers also came in handy thanks to the inclusion of a new item, the fishing rod. Fortnite gamers could now take time out to cast a line into the water and see what they caught – whether it was fish that could replenish health and shields, or weapons!

Towards the end of Chapter One, a house in the central island in the new map started to display some very unusual behavior, turning everything inside it gold. This would prove to be the introduction of the first of the main fortnite Chapter 2 protagonists – Midas.

CHAPTER 2 SEASON 2

At the start of Season 2, there was no sign of Alter and Ego. They were replaced by two warring agencies, Ghost and Shadow. The central island – which had previously been home to nothing much – was turned into a fortress-like building known as The Agency, from which Midas based his operations. Midas was a powerful NPC who turned anything he touched to gold, and as the storyline progressed, it became clear that his ultimate plan was to control the storm that always consumed the island.

Chapter 2 Season 2 was home to a great cameo from DeadPool as well, who showed up after a Ghost member stole his pistols. His party yacht, located off the north east coast of the island, quickly became a hot drop.

Season 2 ended with Midas putting the finishing touches the The Device, a

contraption that he had hoped would help him to control the storm. However, everyone knows that man can never master nature – even men who can turn everything they touch to gold. Midas' attempt to bring the storm under his power failed catastrophically, resulting in the island flooding and huge sections of it sinking underwater.

Intriguingly, it would seem that The Device drew at least some of its power from the Zero Point. During the failed

attempt, we were transported to an alternate dimension where we witnessed Agent Jonesy saying we had seen and heard things we weren't supposed to know about.

Season 2 ended with Midas being consumed by a shark, and the island largely underwater.

CHAPTER 2 SEASON 3

Chapter 2 Season 3 was a largely transitional season that wasn't home to much in the way of storyline revelations. The storm waters that flooded huge parts of the island began to recede week on week, which made for nteresting changes to the map as more and more locations became available again. The waters were now populated by sharks, however and

new water-based areas such as Coral Castle became part of the island.

The most important revelation from Chapter 2 Season 3 was the realisation that The Device was actually the Zero Point itself. Midas' failed attempt to harness its power had left the Zero Point exposed in the wreckage of The

Agency, waiting for someone else to pull it out again.

The Zero Point's power seemed to have seeped into the atmosphere, however, as demonstrated by two astronauts who crashed on the island and used rifts to escape – rifts being portals that transport players to different parts of the map.

Perhaps inevitably, the intense power of the Zero Point drew attention from alternate dimensions and in the sky above the island, the shape of Galactus from the Marvel Cinematic Universe (MCU) began to appear. It soon became clear that Epic was setting us up for a Marvel crossover event, which came to fruition when Thor crashed onto the island to warn of the impending attack, signifying the start of Chapter 2 Season 4.

CHAPTER 2 SEASON 4

This was an official Marvel crossover event, and BOY was it immense! The power of the rifts, which had been hinted at in the previous season, brought a huge chunk of the MCU crashing onto the island – literally. A circular chunk of Manhattan landed in the north-east corner of the map, on top of Frenzy Farm and near to Steamy Stacks. On it was Stark Laboratories as well as Heart Lake and Tony Stark's Lakeside Cabin.

Galactus was drawing nearer and nearer, and the plan was clearly for the Avengers to battle against him to save the island. In Stark's sprawling lab complex, Battle Buses were being prepared for the confrontation, powered by Arc Reactors and led by Tony Stark.

Something big was clearly brewing, and Galactus delivered it at the end of the season. He launched an all-out assault on the island, with the intention of absorbing the Zero Point and its power for himself. The Avengers, led by Stark, launched a counter-attack and managed to defeat Galactus by the skin of their teeth.

The victory, however, was not without a cost. The Zero Point was damaged in the battle, and became unstable. It's incredible power began leaking out, leading to us seeing another cutscene in a different dimension with Agent Jonesy in his office and the whole world shaking violently.

CHAPTER 2 SEASON 5

Chapter 2 Season 5 started through the eyes of Agent Jonesy, as a mysterious woman urged him to use the Zero Point to travel to the island so that he could stabilise it and close any portals leading off the island to other places or dimensions. She told him it was vital that no-one escaped the loop, and also that Jonesy avoided letting the Seven detect his presence.

Of course, Jonesy being Jonesy, he didn't hear the last part of his instructions and leaped into action anyway.

This time the unstable Zero Point brought a desert island crashing down with it, turning the middle of the island into a sandy, desert wasteland. As it appeared, Agent Jones used the Zero Point to summon legendary hunters from a variety of different realms to the island. These included Ripley and the Xenomorph from Aliens, the Mandalorian from the Star Wars Universe, the Predator, the Terminator, Kratos from God of War, and Master Chief from Halo.

Their arrival marked out Chapter 2 Season 5 as the era of the bounty hunter on the island. These cold-blooded contract killers were also part of a shift in the gameplay dynamics, as NPCs (non-playable characters) were now to be found on the island. Some would sell players valuable equipment, while others could be hired to help eliminate other players.

There were also bounty hunter boards, which players could use to take out a bounty on another player. Eliminating that player within the timeframe of the bounty would result in a reward of gold bars, which could be used to buy weapons upgrades and other advantages in game.

As the season drew to a close, Agent Jonesy became angry with the Imagined Order for not helping him to control the Zero Point, which is becoming more and more unstable, and he begins to give consideration that maybe – just maybe – he's backed the wrong side in this conflict...

CHAPTER 2 SEASON 6

The season began with Jonesy containing the explosion of the Zero Point after crushing his coms device, signifying his exit from the Chosen Order. This resulted in reality waves hitting the island, changing the appearance of everyone repeatedly, and when the dust had settled, there were a number of spires dotted around the map, in a star formation, with a large spire at the very centre of the map.

Season 6 threw the island 's technology back in time. A LOOONG way back in time. Titled Primal, it saw the island turn wild, introducing wildlife, primal weapons and primitive crafting techniques into the game. Many of the more futuristic weapons were removed from the game, but the old classics such as shotguns, assault rifle and machine guns remained.

The biggest change on the weaponry front was that sniper rifles were replaced with bows, changing the dynamics of long-range combat significantly. The bows could be crafted into two different directions – mechanical or primal. To craft mechanical items required mechanical parts, which could be found around the island or harvested from vehicles and machinery.

To craft a primal weapon, you would need animal bones, which could be obtained by killing the various wildlife around the map – everything from harmless chickens to terrifying velociraptors and wild wolves!

The bows were definitely where things got really interesting. Once you had a mechanical or primal bow, you could further augment it by combining it with other items. A mechanical bow and grenades could create an explosive bow, where each arrow would fire three grenades after it hit. A primal bow crafted with a petrol can would make a flame bow that would start fires on impact.

There were many different types of bow, but the primal flame bow quickly became one of the most powerful weapons in the game, and a highly desirable addition to any inventory. Not only would it do significant damage with a direct hit, it also rendered elaborate structures useless by turning them from defensive strongholds to fiery deathtraps with just a couple of hits.

CHAPTER 2 SEASON 7

The fantastic thing about Fortnite is that the storyline can move very quickly from one extreme to the other – and so it was the case with Chapter2 Season 7. After a whole season hunting velociraptors and using their bones to upgrade a bow and arrow, Fortnite players were quickly catapaulted into a futuristic scenario as the island came under attack from an altogether new threat – an alien invasion!

From the introductory video for Chapter 2 Season 7, it would seem that the spire towers that had been such a key part of the Primal storyline would ultimately prove the island's downfall. Raz finally managed to get his hands on a spire artifact and, not knowing what it did or how powerful it was, he attracted the attention of a powerful alien race that immediately declared war on the citizens of the island. Nice one, Raz.

A series of crazy alien happenings then followed very quickly – UFO sightings, alien abductions, crop circles and more rocked the island to its very core. It became obvious that the main target for the aliens was the central spire tower.

A huge UFO lowered itself to cover almost the entire island, while the invading alien race successfully infiltrated the Imagined Order and used its own technology to rip the spire tower out of the island. Exactly what happened to the Zero Point remained a mystery, but it could well now be in the hands of the aliens which would give them a huge advantage in the battle for the island's future.

Of course, the citizens of the island did not take this sudden appearance by aliens lightly, and they quickly rallied to fight back. Some warriors from other universes have been dragged in to help win the battle, including Superman himself, but the aliens seem determined, and the battle for the very future of the island began in earnest...

MASTER THE FLYING SAUCER!

CHAPTER 2 SEASON 7 INTRODUCED THE FLYING SAUCER – A TOTALLY NEW VEHICLE FOR FORTNITE FANS TO CONTROL. WE TAKE A LOOK AT THE FEATURES THAT MADE THIS SUCH AN EXCELLENT ADDITION TO THE FORTNITE UNIVERSE AND SHOW YOU HOW TO GET THE MOST OUT OF THIS EXCITING NEW ADDITION.

TAKING A UFO

As you arrive on the map, you'll see that some of the place names are purple in colour. This is where you'll find the Trespassers piloting the saucers. You'll need to shoot the saucer down, which will require you to inflict around 600 damage on it, then kill the Trespasser who jumps out. Once you've accomplished that, the saucer is yours to take! Simply approach the saucer and enter it to take to the skies.

FINDING A UFO

If shooting down a saucer and defeating its pilot in mortal combat sounds like too much hard work for you, then there's always the opportunity to cheat a little and steal one.

Around the map are a number of empty saucers that are being protected by IO guards. By landing at the radar stations, you'll be able to tool up much more quickly with impressive weapons, and the IO guards offer much less of a threat than the Trespassers do. A few well aimed shots to get rid of the IO guards, and a flying saucer with all the alien technology you can handle is yours to do with as you wish!

BATTERY LIFE

We're very used to the vehicles in Fortnite requiring petrol to run, but alien technology is a little more advanced than that, and a whole lot greener to run as well. The saucers rely on a battery that is steadily depleted while you fly. To recharge the battery, you simply need to land the saucer and exit – the battery power will begin to replenish immediately.

Of course this leaves you vulnerable while you're out of the saucer – especially as most other players on the map will have seen where you landed. As a result, it's best to land near to some form of cover so that it's hard for other players to launch an attack or to steal the saucer from you.

The best plan is actually to land on top of a building. You can exit immediately and head inside the building so you're safe from any snipers who have their sights on you. That also means anyone wanting to get to the craft will need to get past you, or laboriously build up the outside of the building. It's far and away the best way to allow your saucer to recover its battery power so you can fly off again to deal some more destruction from above.

TRACTOR BEAM

No self-respecting flying saucer engineer would fail to include the classic tractor beam as a weapon of choice, and you'll be delighted to hear that the boffins at Epic have continued this fine tradition.

The tractor beam works in a pretty traditional way. It is emitted directly beneath the craft and will pick up whatever is in its path. Now, there are a number of different ways that the smart Fortnite player can make the most of that.

The obvious trick is to pick up your opponents and fling them into the storm to cause them damage – it's certainly an effective strategy. However, it's also possible to be a little more cunning.

Instead of targeting other players, it makes a lot of sense to use the tractor beam to pick up rocks or vehicles and then drop them on your opponents or the buildings they have constructed/are hiding in. This can cause a lot more damage than anything you can do directly!

ENERGY BOLT

The saucer can also fire an energy pulse at a target, but this is not an especially brilliant weapon as the shot is slow moving and takes a little while to charge up. A direct hit will cause immediate damage to your target, but even a near miss will result in a burst of energy that can damage nearby structures and – crucially – send opponents flying off in another direction.

Aiming smartly can fire your rivals into the storm causing them significant damage – and you can then continue peppering them as they try to make their way back!

The slow nature both of charging the bolt and its speed once fired, however, mean that it is best used against buildings – and it is here that you can cause some serious damage from the skies.

Rather than looking to take opponents out directly, you should focus instead on spoiling everyone's defensive plans. Take out buildings and defensive structures below you so that those fighting it out down there have nowhere to hide from each other. They'll soon eliminate each other, leaving you with fewer remaining rivals and ensuring that those who do make it through will have taken some damage on the way.

DODGING

As well as the more aggressive moves available to you in the flying saucers, there's also the chance of bursting forward with a sudden jolt of speed for a few metres. This isn't a way to get moving faster because it lasts just a couple of seconds, so instead recognise it for what it is – a great way to dodge shots fired at you from below. In particular, it should become second nature to hit the speed dodge button whenever you see the sky lit up by a rail gun tracer beam.

STANDING ON A SAUCER

The built-in weapons on a saucer aren't going to prove gamechangers on their own. They're good, and they can certainly make a difference, but there may well come a time when you want to use your normal weapons from the higher vantage point that's offered by the flying saucer.

The good news is that doing so is easy – you simply change seat while flying and will move to a position on the outside of the craft, from where you can open fire. The downsides are obvious, in that you are much more exposed to a direct hit yourself.

This move does obviously mean that the saucer will lose altitude, but the good news is that it does so quite slowly. That will give you plenty of opportunities to get a few shots off before you have to head back into the cockpit and fly again.

HOW TO TAKE DOWN A SAUCER

While being in a saucer is a great advantage, it's highly likely you will come under fire from them yourself during the course of your Fortnite career. It's important that you know how to deal with them so that you can seize the initiative back from your airborne rivals if it does happen.

The best weapons to use against a saucer are sniper rifles and rail guns, but the techniques are very different for both. With a sniper rifle, it's all about accuracy (unsurprisingly). You need to aim directly at the player flying the saucer, so shooting straight into the cockpit to eliminate them.

Failing that, you'll need to destroy the craft itself, which is best done with the rail gun. Three successful hits from the rail gun will be enough to bring the saucer down, so you'll

need to be accurate and quick, as well as remembering to move after each shot so the saucer pilot can't track you down.

In both instances, however, you're best off shooting from as close to beneath the saucer as you can risk getting. Shooting directly up gives you the best chance of scoring a hit because the target is larger and it is not moving as much relative to your position. That is a risk, because it involves getting close to the craft and, if the pilot spots you, it's an easy shot for them to cause you some serious damage in return!

PLAY LIKE A PRO:
THE BASICS

IF YOU WANT TO START SEEING VICTORY ROYALES ON A REGULAR BASIS THEN YOU NEED TO FOLLOW SOME BASIC PRO TIPS TO GIVE YOURSELF THE EDGE. WE'RE LIFTING THE LID ON SOME OF THE TECHNIQUES THAT THE BEST FORTNITE PLAYERS AROUND THE WORLD FOLLOW – SO NOW YOU CAN USE THEM TOO!

SMART PAYLOAD

Fortnite gives you five slots in your inventory, so you need to use them wisely. There's absolutely no point in having four shotguns, for example – you need to make sure that you are prepared for all eventualities.

As a rule, it is best to carry a close range weapon (such as a shotgun or submachine gun), a mid-range weapon (such as an assault rifle) and a long-range weapon (such as a sniper rifle or a bow, depending on what's available).

That leaves two slots. One should be reserved for healing items – big health potions or full MedKits take priority here. The other can be used for an explosive weapon (such as grenades, firefly jars, and rocket launchers).

Your next challenge is to make sure you can switch quickly between weapons, so arrange them sensibly! The best solution is usually to have your mid-range weapon placed with your long-range on one side and your short range weapon on the other. Then, if you are in combat you can react to whether your opponent moves closer to you or looks to run away. One further click along should be your explosives, with your healing items on the very outside.

Ideally, always keep the same items in the same slot so that you can train your brain to switch immediately to the right weapon for the right situation without even having to look!

MANAGING YOUR HEALTH

Making the most of the healing items that you find on the island can be a huge part of whether you succeed or fail in battle. You need to reach 100 health and shield as quickly as possible, and get back to full capacity as soon as is sensible after each battle.

The main consumable items – bandages, MedKits and large and small shield potions – should be used wisely. Often you'll find things around you that can help replenish your health and shield without having to use the items you're carrying – ideally you want to keep those for a situation when you are damaged and under fire and have no alternative.

Look out for campfires – they can restore you to 100% health in exchange for stoking them with wood. Similarly,

there are lots of food items around the map that can help you – shield mushrooms, peppers, fruit, meat and more. The specifics change from season to season, but there's always something you can use to make small incremental gains to your health.

You should also look out for slurp trucks and barrels, which can add to your health and shield, while the healing waters around Slurpy Swamp will also help out if you are in that area.

The key is to always see what is nearby before using a MedKit or similar – you can often save those items and keep your health high by being aware of your surroundings and improvising.

LEAVE NOTHING BEHIND

Where you can, try not to leave valuable items behind for your opponents. Open every ammo crate and empty it, even if you've got plenty of bullets. If you find healing items and you're fully loaded try not to leave them behind for someone else to find – if it's safe to do so, pick them up and throw them off a cliff or into a bush to make them harder for other players to get to.

Another useful trick is to build a simple 1X1 wooden box to stop other players seeing the brightly-coloured items from a distance.

They'll often assume it's a discarded healing hut or defensive structure and not investigate further.

Another excellent piece of advice is to light every campfire that you pass, if you have enough wood. This is because it will then burn out, meaning anyone who arrives at it later will need to use 200 wood to light it instead of 30, making it a much less appealing option. This can cause real problems for players who are behind you as you move towards the storm circle, and might mean your opponents arrive in a weaker state than they might otherwise like to.

USE HIGH GROUND

High ground is essential in Fortnite. If you are firing down onto an opponent, you have a much better chance of success than if you are at the bottom of a hill aiming up. Use that to your advantage by always looking to take the higher ground as you move around. Don't wait until you're in a battle because you never know when you'll be taken by surprise – instead, actively seek out the high ground as you move.

However, don't move around on the very peak of the high ground. Doing so means you will be silhouetted against the horizon from both sides, doubling your chances of being spotted and picked off. Instead, move to one side of the peak and move parallel to it. You'll be able to see anyone on the same side as you and have the advantage of that high ground, but you won't be visible to anyone on the other side – perfect!

LAY TRAPS

As well as the in-game traps you can sometimes find in the game (depending on what has been vaulted at any particular time) you can also set your own traps for unsuspecting opponents.

Perhaps the most obvious technique here is lootbaiting – finding lots of weapons that will attract opponents (perhaps from a fallen opponent) and hiding nearby. When an unsuspecting player arrives to pick up the loot, you can leap out from cover and get the drop on them. The same approach also works with loot chests – you can hide nearby and wait for another player to be lured towards them.

You can also use an explosive item such as a gas canister – leave it near to the loot or point of interest that you think will attract players to it, then retreat to a safe distance and line it up in your sights. When an opponent arrives on the scene, it should take only one shot from you to blow them sky high!

DON'T JUST HEAR IT – SEE IT!

The sound in Fortnite is an immersive experience, especially when using headphones. You'll hear sounds to your left and right, and be able to track down enemy gunfire or footsteps accordingly.

However, you don't have to rely on having bat ears to get that advantage. In Fortnite's sound settings there is a setting called 'Visualise Sound Effects'. Once you have that turned on, you'll see footsteps, gunfire, the sound of nearby chests and more, all displayed on the screen. It can be a particular godsend when an enemy is approaching – unless you have your volume set to 100, the odds are you will see the footsteps on screen before you hear them!

CHOOSE YOUR BATTLES

To win a Victory Royale, you only need to be the last person standing. You don't need to rack up 99 kills, so play smart and choose when to engage and when to stay quiet and out of sight.

For example, there's no point in taking pot shots at someone who is miles away. You're unlikely to take them out and will succeed only in giving away your position – both to them and any other nearby players. Instead, wait until you can be sure you'll be able to finish matters quickly before engaging with an opponent!

HOP SKIP AND JUMP!

However smart you try and play, there'll be times when you have no option but to cross an exposed area in order to make it to the storm circle. While you are doing so you'll be a sitting duck for anyone that's got you in their sights – so don't make life easy for them! Avoid moving in a straight line and zigzag left and right instead, so that anyone tracing you won't be able to get an easy shot off. Throw in a few jumps while doing so to become even harder to hit!

PLAY LIKE A PRO: STEALTH

DRAWING ATTENTION TO YOURSELF IN FORTNITE CAN BE A RISKY MOVE, WITH 99 OPPONENTS ALL LOOKING TO TAKE YOU DOWN. HERE ARE SOME TOP TIPS FOR STAYING OUT OF SIGHT TO HELP YOU STAY IN THE GAME FOR LONGER!

FROM COVER TO COVER

If you're looking to play Fortnite in a stealthier way, then you need to apply that to the way you move around the island and how you use cover. Lots of players like to keep moving, but quite simply, the more often you move, the greater the risk of being seen. If you want to play in a stealthy way to make sure you are regularly making the top ten, it is best to move little and often, and to plot your movements so that you are moving from one form of cover to the next.

Once you are in a well-covered location, and you know that you are inside the storm circle, sit tight. There's no need to move; just stay aware of your surroundings and let the other players eliminate each other while you keep out of sight and out of mind. You should only be looking to move as the storm circle shrinks and you need to move to stay inside it – but even then, move very early and find cover as quickly as you can.

HIDE AND SEEK CHAMPION

Knowing where to lay low is an important part of playing like a stealthy pro. Luckily, the island is chock full of excellent hiding places.

Pretty much every building offers somewhere good to hide. The key is to close doors behind you, so passing players have less reason to come and investigate. Once you've made sure the building looks unopened, find somewhere away from a window because there's nothing more annoying than thinking you've found a great hiding spot and being sniped through a window you hadn't taken into consideration!

Next up, make sure you can't be seen from above (so low down in a warehouse is no good – someone can be above you and you'd never know) and that you have a clear vantage point of the entrances to the area. A great place to hide is underneath staircases at the bottom – you usually get lots of noise to

warn you someone is coming down the stairs and you'd be amazed how few players ever check under there.

The other great hiding place in the game is in bushes. Heading into a bush but staying near the edge means you can still see out if you look down the sights of your weapon, so you can spot enemies approaching. You'll often find players will run just yards from you blissfully unaware, giving you an easy finish with a shotgun if you think it's safe to do so.

You can also hide behind trees and boulders, which can be an effective strategy – especially if done on high ground so you can see anyone approaching. Try to stay crouched and hide in the shadow of whatever cover you have chosen if you adopt this approach!

DRESS FOR THE OCCASION

Kitting yourself out is an important part of stealth. You'll get nowhere trying to hide behind a bush while dressed as a six-foot-tall banana, or wearing glowing wings that can be seen from the other side of the island. Choose black or green skins, and avoid colourful back bling, harvesting tools and weapon wraps to give yourself the best chance of not being spotted.

KEEP THE NOISE DOWN

It may sound obvious, but you'll definitely need some quiet weapons that don't give away your location when you fire them. Otherwise, you'll quickly draw unwanted attention to where you are. If you can find, buy or craft silenced weapons, then always do so. Alternatively, use bows or thrown weapons like grenades – your opponents will only hear those when they land and won't necessarily know where they came from!

You also need to minimise the noise you make yourself. For the most part, that means crouching so that others don't hear your footprints, but you should also be wary of switching weapons or reloading too often – the sound it makes can give you away if someone is close by.

COVER OF DARKNESS

Get to know the cycle of life on the island. The days last only a few minutes, so you'll often find that you can wait until night falls before leaving cover and heading somewhere new. If you can move while it's dark, it's always the best time to do it. It will happen gradually so you'll see as dusk approaches and get ready to make your move.

PLAY LIKE A PRO:
UPGRADING

ALTHOUGH THERE ARE LOTS OF WEAPONS IN LOOT CHESTS AND DOTTED AROUND THE ISLAND, THERE WILL BE OCCASIONS WHEN YOU ARE CURSED WITH A SELECTION OF LOW-POWERED WEAPONS TO CHOOSE FROM. IN THOSE INSTANCES, YOU'LL NEED TO KNOW HOW TO UPGRADE THEM QUICKLY AND EFFICIENTLY – SO HERE ARE SOME TOP TIPS!

KNOW WHAT YOU'RE SPENDING

Fortnite varies the mechanisms for upgrading weaponry from season to season, so you need to make sure you understand the costs involved in improving the kit you are already carrying.

Often, an upgrade will require harvested materials to take place. If this is the case, then it is not usually too much of a challenge – you should be looking to upgrade relatively late in the game and by that stage, you'll probably have materials to burn.

If the active upgrading method involves gold, however, you may need to be a little more selective about how often you upgrade your weapons. The costs involved in doing so can be quite steep and really eat away at your gold reserves, so think carefully before you go splashing the cash too much!

PLAY SMART

There are lots of common and uncommon weapons on Fortnite Island, and you'll find plenty of them as you move around the place. As a result, it's generally not worth upgrading weapons at the lower end of the scale. You won't get much bang for your buck – the improvement in performance won't be noticeable enough to make a big difference to your performance.

Instead, try and save your upgrades for turning rare weapons into epic ones, or epic ones into legendary. It costs more, but it actually makes a difference.

CRAFTING ISN'T ALWAYS BETTER!

Often, Fortnite allows you to craft weapons too. This will change the weapon type, using harvested materials, as well as upgrading it to the next level. However, be careful here. You might actually prefer the weapon you start with and be at a disadvantage without it. The quicker fire rate of a tactical shotgun makes it a better weapon than a lever shotgun, for example, even if it is a lower grade. Similarly, many players prefer an assault rifle to a heavy assault rifle, because it is better at distance.

Think carefully about how you manage your crafting and remember that sometimes the best thing to do is leave your weapon choices as they are!

LOOK AROUND

Before you upgrade a weapon, make sure you have scoured all the nearby chests and hunted for any nearby weapons properly. You'll be really annoyed with yourself if you waste gold or materials upgrading a weapon, only to open a nearby Loot Chest and find that the game has just gifted you one. Upgrade benches are usually found in areas that are home to Loot Chests too, so make sure you look thoroughly before upgrading.

CHOOSE THE RIGHT WEAPONS

Sometimes, upgrading a weapon doesn't really make much difference to how much damage it can do, especially considering the circumstances you are likely to use it in. Assault rifles are a good example – the difference between an uncommon version and a legendary version is only 5 extra damage per hit. You'll need to hit an opponent with a full shield seven times at distance to eliminate them with an uncommon weapon, compared to six with a legendary one. The difference in that kind of combat is barely noticeable.

The difference between an uncommon and a legendary pump shotgun, however, is 24 damage. That extra amount can make all the difference, taking an opponent with a full shield down in just two shots instead of three.

As a rule, you get better return on shotguns and pistols, while the sniper rifle also returns a 25 damage improvement at the top end! The trick is to think carefully about which weapons you upgrade and when!

GET IT RIGHT TO START WITH

Upgrading weapons really should be a last resort. It's usually a sign that something has gone badly wrong with your drop – you've either landed in a place with no Loot Chests, or you got there too late and the good weapons have gone!

Getting your drop right means you can avoid having to scrabble around to upgrade weapons altogether, so make that your first priority!

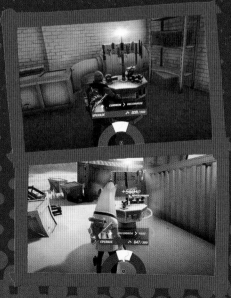

UPGRADING ISN'T ALWAYS BETTER!

In most seasons, you'll find NPCs dotted around the island who you can talk to. Some of these will offer you the chance to upgrade an existing weapon, or even just sell you an epic or legendary weapon (sometimes at very good prices in comparison to the fee of upgrading one!)

Make the most of these opportunities when they arise. As you explore the map, get to know which NPCs offer what, so if you do find yourself in a position where you need to upgrade a weapon, you know where to go.

PLAY LIKE A PRO: VEHICLES

THE ISLAND IS HOME TO LOTS OF DIFFERENT FORMS OF TRANSPORTATION, AND GETTING THE BEST OUT OF THEM

WHEN TO USE A VEHICLE

There are pros and cons to using the vehicles in Fortnite. While they obviously enable you to move from one area to another quickly, they do generate a LOT of noise and alert opponents to your location, even if they are quite a distance away. As such, be careful about overusing vehicles, especially in the later stages of the game. In a small storm circle, you'll just make it easy for them to find you.

Instead, you're best off reserving the use of vehicles for fairly early in the game, especially if you find yourself a long way from the storm circle and time is running out. The chances of giving your position away are slimmer as the players are spread out over a larger area, so it's less of a risk. If you're unlucky and find your landing spot is a long way from the storm circle, then it makes even more sense.

FIRING FROM A VEHICLE

You can fire from some vehicles while you drive them, which makes them a really useful feature. The motorboat's rocket launcher can do bags of damage, for example – both in terms of hitting opponents or blowing their buildings or cover to smithereens.

However, what lots of Fortnite players DON'T know is that you can shoot from other vehicles that don't have built in weapons – cars and choppers, for example. You can't shoot while you are driving, but you CAN shoot if you swap seats. Quickly swap seats and aim at your target, before swapping back into the driving seat and fleeing the scene!

This technique isn't the easiest, so don't expect to be sniping enemies from distance while your car coasts driverless down a hill or your chopper starts dropping from the sky – but if you have a rocket launcher, grenades or other explosive weapons in your inventory, you can do some serious damage!

THE BATTERING RAM

If you drop and roll while a vehicle is moving, it will carry on in a straight line until it loses momentum. You can use this to your advantage, turning the car or truck into a battering ram.

The technique is simple enough – accelerate towards a building or bush where opponents are hiding. A few yards before impact, jump out and draw your weapon. The vehicle will smash through walls, trees or bushes and can often leave your opponent without cover. If you're quick on the trigger you can make the most of that opportunity!

THE MOBILE EXPLOSIVE

Vehicles will also explode if they take too much of a beating, and this in turn will damage anyone who happens to be standing close by. Make the most of this – leave a vehicle near to a pile of loot and make sure you have damaged it so it only has a couple of hits left before it explodes.

Retreat to a safe vantage point and wait for someone to come to collect the loot. A couple of well-placed shots at the vehicle will see it explode, and may well eliminate your opponent in the process. You can even use this technique in a moving vehicle, like the battering ram approach. With a damaged vehicle, jump out and let it coast towards an opponent, then shoot at it so it explodes!

WEAPON SELECTION

When you exit a vehicle, you'll be carrying the same weapon you were holding when you first got in (assuming you were driving). Make sure you've selected something sensible so you're ready for battle the moment you leave it – you'll feel very foolish if you med up then leap into a car, only to jump out and threaten an opponent with a MedKit later in the game!

FILL HER UP!

Remember that vehicles need petrol to keep going. Check how much they have in the tank before getting in – if you need to use a petrol tank to fill up then do it, or drive to a nearby petrol station and use that. Sometimes it's better to take a less favourable vehicle with a full tank than something you'd rather use that's running on fumes – especially if you are trying to outrun the storm!

KNOW THE ISLAND

The first thing you need to do is make sure you know the island really well. Just knowing what's in the named locations isn't enough – you need to spend some time in the early stages of each new season getting to know what's NOT on the map – points of interest near to named locations can make excellent starting points, or great back-up plans (more on those later).

Make sure you explore thoroughly, in Battle Lab mode if you like. Loot Chests, Llamas and Ammo Boxes will spawn randomly, but there is a pattern to them and you'll find most of them appear more often than not – so find locations where there's a high probability that you'll be able to stock up with weapons very quickly.

PLAY LIKE A PRO: LANDING

LANDING IN THE RIGHT PLACE CAN MAKE THE DIFFERENCE BETWEEN A VICTORY ROYALE AND BEING THE FIRST PLAYER TO LEAVE THE GAME! OUR GUIDE HELPS YOU MAKE SMART CHOICES EVERY TIME!

HAVE MULTIPLE OPTIONS

Depending on the route of the battle bus and where other players are landing, you'll probably need to choose three or four regular landing spots. Remember, the more you land in the same places, the better drilled you'll become at each and the greater your chances of victory become. Make sure that you know these places like the back of your hand, so that you can react quickly – especially if a Loot Chest that's usually in a certain location hasn't spawned. Knowing where else you might find one can be a real life saver.

Make sure these are spread sensibly around the map – ideally one towards each corner makes the most sense, as it gives you the widest choice.

USE HIGH GROUND

Your glider will automatically open at a certain height, but you can use that to your advantage too. If you're coming in over the outside of the map but heading towards a mountain, your glider will open and you can glide towards the side of the mountain. That will be higher than the ground below you was, so you'll have boots on the ground quicker – and in the opening stages of a Battle Royale, seconds can make a big difference. You can use the same trick to land on the tops of buildings and break in via the roof, too!

GET YOUR TIMING RIGHT

As you come into land, you really need to get your timing right. Make sure you've marked your landing location on the map before the game starts, so you have a guide to how far away you are. Pop your chute around 500 meters from the landing spot and glide in, but keep looking around you for other players. Remember that Loot Chests and weapons that are on the ground will glow, so you can see them as you approach. Try to time things so that you land next to something you can pick up quickly – not having a weapon in your hands within 5 seconds is one of the biggest mistakes newbies make, and it usually means a pretty quick end to your game!

INTERCEPT LATECOMERS

Once you are on the ground and you have a weapon in your hands, listen out for the sound of other players gliding into land nearby, and look up to see if you can spot any. If you can, head over to them as they land to eliminate them immediately or, if you're a good enough shot, blast them out of the air before they even get their feet on solid ground!

HAVE A BACKUP PLAN

As you get close to your intended landing area, you might find that things are just a little too hot for your liking. If that's the case, then you should have another landing spot nearby in mind. This is where exploring the map and knowing your landing spots really well can be invaluable, because you'll only know your plans are changing when you pop your chute! Again, there's no substitute for practice and exploration here!

PLAY LIKE A PRO:
TEAMWORK

PLAYING SOLO IS ONE THING, BUT YOU NEED A SLIGHTLY DIFFERENT SKILLSET WHEN IT COMES TO STEPPING INTO TEAM-BASED COMBAT ON THE ISLAND. HERE ARE SOME WAYS TO MAKE SURE YOUR DUO, TRIO OR SQUAD HAS THE EDGE!

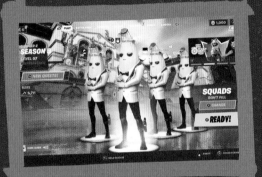

PRACTICE MAKES PERFECT

Playing multiplayer is a very different experience to a solo Battle Royale, so don't expect to just drop into a squads game and find everything easy. You need to play duos, squads or trios regularly in order to improve, so be prepared to put some time in. The skills you learn in solo are useful, but they need to be modified.

Try to play with the same friends on a regular basis. If you have classmates you can play with then even better – you'll learn each other's strengths and weaknesses and get to know everyone's different styles. This can make all the difference – the more often you can play with the same group of friends, the better the experience will become!

COMMUNICATION IS KEY

It's essential that you all know what the other is planning to do. If you are playing with people that you know, then this is exactly what the headset was invented to! Get in a group and talk; you'll be able to share so much more information that way.

If you're playing with strangers and not in a group chat, then use the in-game communication system to make it clear what the plan is. Set waypoints you can all head towards, tag enemies for each other, and point out discarded weapons that might be of use to your teammates.

ROLES AND RESPONSIBILITIES

It's best to try and specialise as best you can, so that each player is playing to their strengths. Again, this is easiest when you are playing with the same group of people repeatedly. For example, if you have an expert archer or sniper in your ranks, make sure they have the right weapons and – crucially – enough ammunition. There's no point in one of you carrying sniper ammo when your sniper runs out, for example.

You also need to work together to make the most of inventory slots as a group. It's silly for three players to each take up a slot with a MedKit, for example, when one player can carry three. That frees up two slots within the squad for other weapons to be carried.

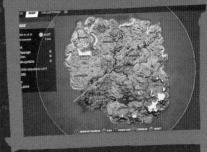

DROP SMART

The quickest way to get eliminated in team-based modes is by dropping alone, away from your squad. Instead, nominate a landing point on the map and drop near to each other. There's no point all landing in the same spot a couple of metres apart, as there won't be enough weaponry to go round – instead choose locations with a decent number of Loot Chests and take one each so that you start the match tooled up and close to each other. If you do split up, try and do so into two pairs, or a pair and a single player, rather than everyone being on their own.

FLANK YOUR OPPONENTS

The best way of working as a group is for one or two players to draw the attention of your opponents while the others sneak round the side of them. When encountering another squad, build or find some cover and fire at them. While their attention is focused on the incoming bullets, use any available cover or the curve of the land to sneak out and to the left or right. Arc your way around quietly (while crouching) before popping up and getting in some unopposed shots on your opponents!

THE AMBUSH

Another great tactic is for most of the group to hide in a bush or building, leaving just one member as 'cannon fodder'. That player should attract the attention of nearby players by making noise, firing at them from a distance and generally acting like a total noob. When the other squad rushes in, thinking they've got an easy elimination on their hands, everyone springs out of hiding and takes them by surprise!

PLAY LIKE A PRO:
BUILDING

BECOMING A PROFICIENT BUILDER CAN ABSOLUTELY MAKE THE DIFFERENCE BETWEEN WINNING AND LOSING WHEN YOU GET TO THE FINAL FEW PLAYERS. ALL THE PROS ARE GREAT BUILDERS, SO IT'S IMPORTANT THAT YOU BECOME ONE TOO.

START AT THE BEGINNING

Although you will probably only be building big structures towards the end of the game, you need to start planning for that from the start. Gather materials at every opportunity, harvesting what you can while it is safe to do so. Once you've established that the area around your landing zone is clear and you've got some weapons, it is safest to start this in the first storm circle because the players are spread out over a wider area and there is less chance of anyone hearing or seeing you.

Wood is abundant throughout the game but it won't last long under sustained fire in those closing rounds, so take any opportunity you can to harvest stone and metal. Interior walls and staircases are great as they don't leave you exposed to fire from anyone outside. Also remember to preserve these supplies for later in the game – for smaller, temporary structures such as healing huts or shields, use wood.

QUICK BUILDS

Master the art of the quick build item, and use wood to do it. From time to time you'll need to throw a quick shield wall up when you come under fire from a distance, or to build a small hut with a roof on so you can med up safely. You may also need to build ramps to enter buildings at a higher level, or to quickly scale the sides of mountains or cliffs. These are valuable ways to learn the skills you need for building bigger, stronger structures and will come in handy.

CHOOSE YOUR TIME WELL

You don't want to leave building until the very last minute, but starting too soon can mean you have to leave it if the storm circle moves. Ideally, wait until the last four or five players remain then build a mid-sized stone structure a couple of stories high. When the storm circle closes in, you'll know where you stand. If you are still inside it, you can add to what you have – if you need to move, you haven't wasted too many materials.

STRONG BUILDS NEED STRONG BASES

The key to a good building that you can use in combat is to avoid a single point of failure. If your entire build has only one or two pieces in contact with the floor, it will be easy to destroy. Any opponent with a brain will shoot out those bottom parts and watch the whole thing fall to the ground.

Instead, build sturdy bases from metal or stone. Rather than a simple 1x1 square, try and build at least a 2x1 rectangle so that your opponents have more pieces to shoot out.

USE THE RAMP

Avoid sticking your head above the top of your structure until you know where your opponent is – and use the third person perspective to look for them without revealing yourself! You'll be able to pop into sight already having a bead on them, so you can fire a couple of shots then duck back down again!

BUILDING HIGHER

Always build ramps with a wall in front of them as you go up. That means your opponent will need to shoot out two pieces - the protective wall, then the ramp you are standing on. If you just build ramps, you'll be shot out much quicker!

PLAY LIKE A PRO: EXPLOSIVES

THERE ARE PLENTY OF GUNS IN FORTNITE, BUT THE REAL PROS OUT THERE COMBINE THEM WITH EXPLOSIVE WEAPONS IN ORDER TO CAUSE MAXIMUM DAMAGE TO THEIR OPPONENTS. HERE'S HOW THEY DO IT.

DIRECT HIT

The obvious way to take out an opponent with explosives is via the direct hit. This isn't always easy with grenades or rocket launchers however, as they give a reasonable amount of warning – in fact, a direct hit with a rocket launcher is a pretty rare event. To counter the warning of hissing grenades (which can give an opponent time to start running!) throw them in bunches. Ideally, collect 6 (the most you can have in a single slot) and throw them all in an arc shape. If you time it right (and with a little practice, you will!) your opponent should find themselves running away from one explosive but directly into another!

GRENADING TECHNIQUES

A great way to use grenades from height is to simply drop them at the top of a cliff where an opponent awaits at the bottom. The grenade will roll down the hill and by the time they hear that fateful hissing sound it will be too late – the grenade will be about to detonate as it hits the ground halfway through its journey and rolled the rest of the way!

This tactic can also work if your opponent has a wall or cliff face behind them. Rather than worrying about a direct hit, throw your grenade into the

wall and let it drop down to do the damage!

On a similar note, be careful when throwing grenades up at a higher opponent. If you are doing so, make sure you don't aim too close to the cliff face because if you mistime it and hit the cliff face, that grenade is coming right back to join you.

DESTROYING COVER

Explosives are far more useful when it comes to destroying an opponent's cover. By using grenades or rockets wisely, you can leave them defenceless. To master this technique, you'll need to switch quickly to another weapon to follow up the explosion with a volley of gunfire. Keeping your explosives in the slot next to an automatic weapon makes this much easier to accomplish.

THE DISTRACTION TECHNIQUE

When something goes bang, people tend to look in that direction. Use that to your advantage. Rather than throwing a grenade at your opponent, aim for something a few yards to their left or right. When they investigate the explosion, you can leave your cover and finish them off with your other weapons.

IF YOU CAN'T STAND THE HEAT

Some explosive devices, such as an exploding petrol can or a flaming arrow, can set fire to wood. This can be a huge advantage, especially against opponents who are hiding inside buildings. By igniting something flammable on a wooden floor or wall, you can burn through cover in seconds. This has two useful effects on your opponent. Firstly, if they come into contact with fire, they will sustain damage. Secondly, they will need to move, and quickly, to escape the burning building – and you can be ready to greet them with a shotgun in your hand! Don't forget that as well as wooden buildings, this trick will also set fire to trees, bushes and grass.

CAUGHT IN A TRAP!

If you think ahead, you can set some fantastic explosive traps for your opponents in the game. As well as weapons like timed explosives or proximity mines (which are often vaulted for long periods) you can also make your own explosions. It's best attempted in conjunction with lootbaiting – leave a badly damaged car and/or a petrol can near a load of goodies and wait. When your opponents approach it, you shoot the car or can and suddenly, everything goes boom!

PLAY LIKE A PRO: HIRED HELP

ALTHOUGH FORTNITE IS OFTEN SEEN AS A SOLITARY EXPERIENCE, YOU CAN HIRE AI CHARACTERS IN THE GAME TO MAKE YOUR TASK A LITTLE EASIER. HERE'S OUR PRO GUIDE TO THE DOS AND DON'T OF RECRUITMENT!

TAMING AND HACKING

This technique tends to rely on characters (or animals) that spawn randomly on the island (though you can often guess where they are likely to appear). You do need to plan ahead though, and carry meat if you want to tame wolves and corn if you want to get some boar on side. That way, when you run into them, you'll be ready. Of course, that leaves you fewer slots in your inventory, so ideally you want to tame animals as quickly as you can, then restock with extra weaponry.

If the game reintroduces characters that can be hacked, you don't need to be prepared in advance and can just go for it when you encounter them. Remember that you can only have a maximum of three followers at any time though!

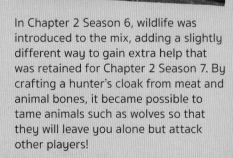

DIFFERENT GAME MODES

As a rule, you get more value from recruiting extra help in Solo than in any other game mode. While you can still recruit in Duos, Trios and Squads, the extra pair of hands is not as much use. Indeed, they can often get in the way of any carefully-laid plans you try to execute. Remember in multiple player modes, the NPC will be linked to the player that hired/hacked/tamed them – if you die, they die, and they will follow that particular player if the group splits up and moves in different directions.

DIFFERENT TYPES OF HELP

There are two very different ways in which you can pull in a little bit of help. The first is to find an NPC who can be hired in exchange for a few gold bars, while the second is to find in-game opportunities to hire multiple players who are often fulfilling a purpose in the game already. In the past these have included hacking Stark Robots and hiring First Order Stormtroopers when they are encountered in the game – instead of shaking them down, you could approach them when they were knocked and hack them.

In Chapter 2 Season 6, wildlife was introduced to the mix, adding a slightly different way to gain extra help that was retained for Chapter 2 Season 7. By crafting a hunter's cloak from meat and animal bones, it became possible to tame animals such as wolves so that they will leave you alone but attack other players!

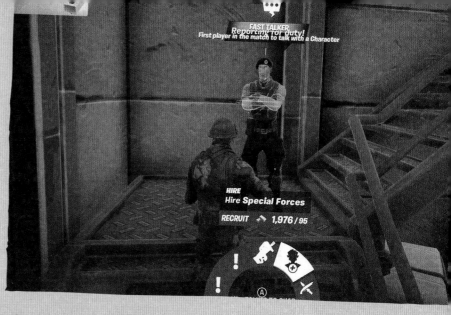

RECRUITING NPCS

Getting one of the main characters from the game is definitely a smart move if you can manage it. It will cost you gold, but if you rack up a few eliminations and survive into the game a while you'll often make most of it back anyway.

This is something that is best done very early on in the game – try to identify where the hirable NPCs are on the map (for example, in Chapter 2 Season 7 there was only one – Special Forces, who could be found at Catty Corner) and land near them. Grab a weapon or two quickly and then get hiring, before anyone else can get to them! It makes far more sense to hire an NPC like this as soon as possible in the game if you are going to make it a key part of your tactics – though that's not to say you shouldn't hire one if you find yourself meeting one relatively late in the game.

USING RECRUITMENT TO YOUR ADVANTAGE

Quite simply, anyone you recruit should be used to attract enemy fire. Try to stay out of sight yourself as much as possible, and let your opponent engage in a firefight with your helper. While they are distracted, you can flank them and often take them down with comparative ease. Don't leave your helper fighting alone for too long though – they will get killed fairly quickly if you don't step in.

THE DISADVANTAGES

If stealth is your thing, then having a helper might get on your nerves. The AI isn't the brightest and you'll often find your buddy will open fire on opponents when they are miles away to draw attention to your position or – more annoyingly – take a dislike to a structure you are hiding behind or in and destroy it! You need to be flexible if you are playing with a recruited character, and be prepared to change your plans if they ruin things!

CHAPTER 2 SEASON 7 EXPOSED

CHAPTER 2 SEASON 7 INTRODUCED SOME AMAZING NEW TWISTS TO THE FORTNITE UNIVERSE! READ ON TO GET THE INSIDE TRACK ON THE BIGGEST NEW DEVELOPMENTS!

IO GUARDS

One of the big changes sees the return of the IO guards, representatives of the Imagined Order. This time round, they are defending satellite stations that are presumably monitoring the communications and movements of the aliens.

They are a grumpy bunch who will open fire pretty much as soon as they see you, but you really don't need to worry about them too much. They are lumbering, slow, and horrible shots – as well as lacking in pretty much any intelligence.

The easiest way to get the better of the IO guards is to make sure you are higher or lower than them. They really struggle to deal with this, and find it much harder to shoot up or down stairs than they really should. This will give you ample opportunity to take them down. They are usually carrying decent weapons as well, even though they never seem to think to use them to defend themselves!

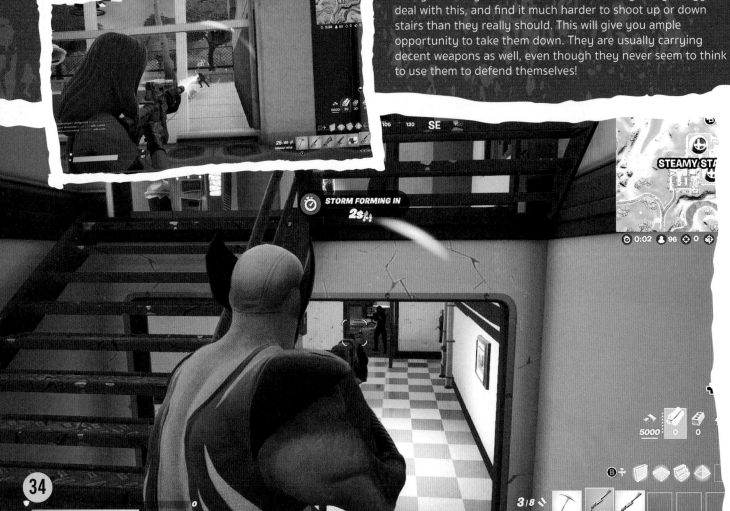

THE RECON GUN

This is a cracking new addition to the weapons available in Fortnite. It doesn't do any damage, but instead it fires a sensor towards whatever you are aiming at. That sensor will send a pulsing blue light out in a dome shape around its resting place, revealing any opponents (in a red outline) or Loot Chests, ammo boxes etc (in a yellow outline).

It will reveal them through walls and defensive structures for as long as the sensor is pulsating (about 20 seconds or so) which is long enough for you to hatch a plan to either avoid or eliminate the opponents it reveals.

It can also be useful when deciding whether to enter a building that is a little distance away – as well as assuring you that it is uninhabited and therefore safe to approach, it can also tell you whether or not the place has already been ransacked or not and whether it's worth the effort getting there or not.

THE RAIL GUN

Another new weapon for Chapter 2 series 7, the rail gun sends a pulse of light and energy at your opponent. It can cause a massive amount of damage, but that comes at a cost – it also sends a solid red beam of light towards the target before it fires a shot, and the beam is still visible for a few seconds after the shot.

That means that anyone nearby will see where the shooter was, making it an easy way to give away your position. As such, you should only use this if you are confident there are no opponents too close to you, and you should move to a new location after firing it just to be on the safe side.

If you see the dreaded beam of light targeting you, you need to be quick! The best solution, if you cant get behind cover, is to build a wall quickly. It will absorb most of the blast, giving you the chance to get away, collect your thoughts, and decide your next move.

The rail gun is especially useful against vehicles. Even the flying saucers, which seem almost impossible to bring down with normal weapons, will only survive a handful of hits. It's utterly useless, however, in close range combat because it takes so long to charge. By the time it's ready to fire, you'll probably be looking at the loading screen for your next match...

UFOS

Another huge change is the inclusion of flying saucers. These spawn in different locations each time, but there's always a clue – look at the location names while you are on the battle bus. The saucers will be circling at the locations with purple names.

There'll be three saucers in each location. In order to board one, you'll need to shoot it down, then defeat the Trespasser NPC that is flying it. Once you've accomplished that (no mean feat) you'll be able to clamber into the UFO and pilot it yourself. They can take a little getting used to, but they have some excellent weaponry that can give you an edge in combat. However, they aren't the speediest of vehicles and you might find yourself under fire. Luckily for you, we've got a detailed guide to flying saucers on page 10!

THE PULSE RIFLE

Another new weapon for Chapter 2 Season 7 is the pulse rifle, which is usually found in the possession of IO guards or in the chests around their base. It fires a single pulse of energy and is reasonably effective – as well as being accurate at long distance.

It can also be useful at close range if you don't look down the sight. Not using the sight enables the weapon to pulse out shots much quicker, at around three times the rate. This makes it a decent addition to the inventory because it can cover more than one type of combat – though it should be noted that it is not as good at either distance as a specialist weapon.

FIREFLIES

The fireflies are still an important part of Chapter 2 Season 7. They proved their work in the previous season, but they are more valuable than even now in the absence of flame bows. A well-aimed firefly jar can ignite the hiding place of an opponent, forcing them into the open or even causing them enough damage to eliminate them directly.

BATTLE PASS CHANGES

One of the most interesting changes that Chapter 2 Season 7 introduced was a free, less restricted Battle Pass system. Previously in Fortnite, this was completely linear – you would unlock set rewards at each evel.

Chapter 2 Season 7 changed that by introducing different pages as you progress through the Battle Pass. You need to reach a certain level or to have unlocked a number of items from previous pages before you could move on, but the exact order you then unlock items in is up to you. You get 5 Battle Stars for each level you increase by, and you can spend them on whichever reward you like.

There are cheaper items available, such s basic emotes for three stars, while the skins and more impressive items increase in price. Some items require you to have purchased others first. If you're looking to unlock as many pages as you can, focus on the cheaper items as unlocking later levels is dependent on how many items you have unlocked – cheaper items means a higher figure for that.

WILDLIFE

The wildlife that was introduced as part of Chapter 2 Season 6 is still running around the map (no raptors though!) but it works a little differently now. They no longer drop animal bones that enable you to craft weapons, though they still drop meat that will recover a small amount of health (often useful after an attack by wolves as they can cause a fair amount of damage!)

In addition, they now drop shield mushrooms, which will increase your shield when consumed. It means that they are well worth keeping an eye out for, especially if you have a silenced weapon that won't draw attention to your position.

GOLD LIMIT

Gold supplies are capped at 5,000 bars now. It used to be 10,000 but that changed in Chapter 2 Season 6, and the lower limit has been retained ever since. With that in mind, there's no point in stockpiling forever! Use that gold every so often to upgrade weapons – it makes room for you to pick more up later on in the game. Keep an eye on your balance though – if you drop below 2,000 it may be worth focusing on completing quests until it's back to a healthier level at around 4,000.

TELEPHONE QUESTS

Another new addition in Chapter 2 Season 7 comes in the form of telephones that ring to offer you additional challenges. Successfully complete them and you'll be rewarded with gold bars that you can use to upgrade weapons or hire NPCs amongst other things.

Get into the habit of answering the phone at every opportunity to accept the challenges on offer. You have literally nothing to lose – if you fail, there are no repercussions. If you succeed, however, you'll be rewarded with those lovely gold bars.

You'll usually be given a couple of options when you answer the phone – typically one quest to be completed within an hour, or another quest to be completed during that specific game. Choose carefully, depending on the situation. If you're down to the final ten and have the offer of a qeust that requires three eliminations in that game, for example, it's probably pointless accepting it. Try to look for quests that will give you more time to complete them, and that tie in with your own skills – if you're hopeless with a sniper rifle then there's no point accepting a sniper challenge, for example.

HIDDEN CASH

As well as challenges and quests, you can also bolster your supplies of gold bars in less obvious ways. In particular, destroying sofas and beds very often yields a return of gold bars, so never leave any standing.

Another handy hint – and it's amazing how many players don't know this – is to search the cash registers that you find in the many shops and restaurants on the island. They always contain gold bars, so get into the habit of checking them all so you increase your bank balance as you go!

BOUNTY HUNTER

Dotted around the board you'll find various bounty boards. Approaching them will trigger a bounty, where you can hunt down one of your opponents and earn a gold bar reward if you eliminate them within the time limit.

These are another hangover from Chapter 2 Season 6 and again, they are well worth your time. You lose nothing if you fail to complete them, and you even get a reward if another player eliminates your target. If nothing else, you get to see roughly on the map where at least one of your opponents is, which can be quite handy – especially in the later stags of the game.

MONSTER TRUCKS!

Another new aspect in Chapter 2 Season 6 that is still in the game is the ability to mod cars by adding oversize tyres to them. This gives whichever vehicle you fit the tyres to the ability to climb pretty much anything – even sheer rock faces that are completely impassable on foot.

You'll usually find the tyres in garages – either at gas stations or residential garages – and they are nearly always near a car as well. If you carry the tyres with you, they take up a slot in your inventory which isn't very efficient so it's best to deploy them on a nearby car as soon as you see a set. Make sure that the car you choose has plenty of petrol

in it (or that you refuel it) and then you have a ready-made escape vehicle if you need it.

The ability to head up mountains is especially useful if you are trying to outrun the storm, but be warned – it does slow the vehicle down tremendously so you might still take some damage. Overall though, it's a great way to get around the map without having to worry too much about things like roads.

There's also a cheeky way you can use the tyres as a weapon – though carrying them round in your inventory still isn't really recommended. If you throw them at an opponent, you can bounce them back into the storm!

FORTNITE'S HIDDEN SECRETS

ONE OF THE COOLEST THINGS ABOUT FORTNITE IS THAT EPIC IS ALWAYS HIDING THINGS IN THE GAME. SOME OF THESE ARE CULTURAL REFERENCES TO THINGS OUTSIDE THE GAME, AND SOME OF THEM ARE COOL HIDDEN LITTLE EXTRAS THAT YOU MIGHT NOT KNOW ABOUT! HERE ARE SOME OF OUR FAVOURITES!

CENTRAL ISLAND

After the drama of the start of Chapter 2, not many people noticed that the small island in the middle of the new map looked familiar. In fact, it was the same shape as the original island – the one that had just been zapped into the ether!

The map has changed a few times now in Chapter 2 so it is no longer there in the same form, but those original gamers who missed the old island certainly appreciated the nod to history back at the start of the bold new era!

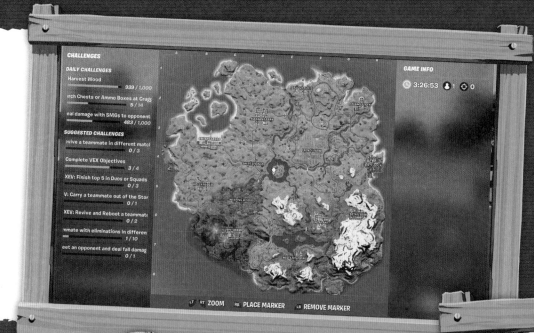

HOMER WORKS HERE!

At the start of Chapter 2, anyone heading to Steamy Stacks found a rather delicious hidden extra. The huge cooling towers of Steamy Stacks remind us of a certain nuclear power plant overlooking a little town called Springfield, pumping all sorts of nastiness into the air breathed by Homer, Marge, Bart and Lisa. As we all know, Homer is a (reluctant) employee at the plant. Visiting the main office block, on the eastern side of Steamy Stacks, revealed that someone has left some delicious-looking donuts on one of the machines there. At the time of going to press, they were still there and seem to be a permanent feature! Go for yourself and check out this cool easter egg (or should that be easter donut?).

RINGING DOORBELLS

Eve the Fortnite island isn't out of reach of the postal service. Or Amazon, probably. To make sure the residents know that their delivery is here – a purple shotgun, perhaps,or a multipack of small shields – you'll see that lots of the houses have a doorbell out the front. If you approach these and use the action button, you'll find that you can ring the doorbell. This can draw attention to your position if anyone is on the building, but it can also act as a useful diversion – ring the front door, then run round to the back door to catch them by surprise.

You can even break a doorbell by pressing it repeatedly – you'll be rewarded with a puff of smoke and a mournful final 'ding dong' as it breaks. That means the resident would have to order a new one from Amazon – but then how would they know it's arrived?

RIDING THE FIRE HYDRANTS

In a lot of the urban areas around the map, you'll notice that the houses have fire hydrants outside. Safety first, after all – no-one wants a fire (even if your home does regularly come under attack from rocket launchers and grenades…) These are much more than decoration, however!

Fire a shot or swing your harvesting tool while targeting a fire hydrant, and you'll knock the top off. What happens to all that pressurised water once there's nothing holding it back? You guessed it – a jet of water fires into the air.

This water jet is not just pretty to look at – it can offer you a competitive advantage if you know what you are doing. By standing on top of the jet, you'll be propelled into the air – not too far, about one storey high. However, that's plenty enough to enable you to reach a roof or upstairs balcony, enabling you to enter a building at the first floor level and bypassing the front door altogether.

You can even use fire hydrants along with the doorbell – ring the doorbell so your opponent thinks you're at ground level, then leap on a water jet and enter the building from above to get them from behind while they investigate the front door…

SCORE A GOAL

When the residents of the island aren't armed to the teeth and engaging in a 100-player Battle Royale, they love nothing more than a kickabout. That reputation was underlined by the visit of Neymar to the island in Chapter 2 Season 6, but the history of football on the island dates back far earlier than that!

The footballs you see around the island (and the beach balls you find on the beach too, for that matter) can all be kicked around. In fact, there are some fan-made games based entirely around playing football! However, not everyone knows that scoring a goal on the island will result in a little fanfare and the scoreboard updating too!

You'll find the football pitch at Pleasant Park, with a goal at either end – if you score at different ends then you'll see the scoreboard updates accordingly. Be careful though, as other players will hear the sound if you score and it can draw attention to your position – though it's still a pretty cool little hidden extra!

GATHER ROUND THE CAMPFIRE

A lot of players know that they can use the campfires around the map to heal themselves. Simply approach one and light it – you can also stoke it for 30 wood to heal a little quicker. So far, so straightforward, right?

However, what lots of players forget is that they can light campfires even when they have 100 health. It won't give you any benefits to your health, so what's the point you may well think. Well, once a campfire has been lit and burned out, it will cost another player 200 wood to restock it and light it again. That's a lot of wood!

By lighting the campfires as you leave an area, you can make it more difficult for other players to use them. This is an especially handy technique if you are moving away from the storm – those behind you won't be able to use the campfires to heal themselves, so they will waste any health items they have instead (or be eliminated if they don't have any).

Be careful though as the smoke might give you away – if you aren't using the fire to heal, then move away from it as quickly as possible to avoid anyone finding you.

LONG DISTANCE VISION

No matter how big your television is, sometimes you just can't make out what items are if they are a long way away. This can be really frustrating, especially if you can see that there is a stash of items nearby, but you can't see what it is. No-one wants to take a risk crossing open space to get to some loot only to discover that it is just a basic pistol and a load of ammunition.

So, short of buying an even bigger television or playing with your nose two inches from the screen, how can you work around this problem? The answer is simple – and delightfully sneaky. Look down your sights at the discarded item and tag it. It will now show up in an information circle on your HUD, telling you exactly what it is you are pointing at. For multiple items just move a little left or right each time and repeat.

Using this approach, you can quickly and easily see whether it is worth leaving your cover and going in pursuit of a bigger and better payload, or whether you should just sit tight and let others squabble over who gets it!

FERRIS BUELLER'S DAY OFF

Way back in the murky depths of time (1986 to be precise), one of the biggest films of the year was Ferris Bueller's Day Off. In the film, Bueller (played by Matthew Broderick) skips school with his friend Cameron and tries to impress his girlfriend Sloane.

A big part of the film focuses on Cameron's dad's car – a 1961 Ferrari Spyder and his pride and joy. Ferris 'borrows' the car for a day of fun for the threesome around Chicago, and returns it, remarkably undamaged, at the end of the day. However Cameron resents the way that his father lavishes so much care and attention on the car, and gets so angry he kicks the vehicle. Unfortunately, in doing so, he knocks it off the jack it was supported on and it plunges through the plate glass window of the his luxurious family house, smashing into the trees outside.

What's this got to do with Fortnite? Well, someone at Epic is also a Ferris Bueller fan because the house from that iconic scene popped up as part of the Chapter 2 refresh. It was under construction in the first three seasons, and by the fourth it was completed and even home to a red car looking just a little like that Ferrari Spyder.

Pay it a visit – it's in the northwest of the map, not too far from Sweaty Sands!

GOLDEN WONDER!

As well as the usual building materials, Fortnite has reintroduced the use of gold as a form of in-game currency. You can use gold bars to hire NPCs, buy goodies from vending machines, and upgrade your weapons. Usually, you'll increase your supply of gold bars by taking them from beaten opponents or by completing quests.

However, there are other ways to boost your bank balance! You'll find gold bars by smashing up sofas and washing machines, which leave gold behind as well as the materials you'll harvest. You can also find gold by searching shop tills in the game!

SICKEST

ONE OF FORTNITE'S STAND-OUT FEATURES IS THE HUGE RANGE OF DIFFERENT SKINS AVAILABLE IN THE GAME. COMBINING THEM WITH BACK BLING MEANS THAT YOU CAN EXPRESS YOUR OWN CREATIVITY IN A WAY THAT IS TOTALLY YOU.

Skins tend to cost V-Bucks, but if you want to expand your choice of skins without breaking the bank, then investing in a Battle Pass is the way forward. You'll automatically unlock skins as you go, and earn enough V-Bucks through the Battle Pass to buy the next one too (as long as you reach level 100 before the season ends).

Remember though, that the skins don't really offer any advantage in the game. Some may offer better camouflage than others, but the original skins do a pretty good job of that anyway. So don't feel that you HAVE to buy skins – they are a fun extra, as you'll see here, but they won't make you any better or worse at the game itself.

FOOD AND DRINK

Some of the best skins in Fortnite are reserved for things to eat and drink. If you're feeling peckish, you could always start out with one of these skins!

BEEF BOSS

Classification: Epic
Price: 1,400

Beef Boss is based on the design of one of the island's restaurants – Durr Burger. Sadly his restaurant is no longer running, but you can still relive the glory days by choosing this skin for battle.

BEEF BOSS
Victory well done.
Part of the **Durrr Burger** set.
Introduced in **Season 5**.

1,500

PURCHASE ITEMS
BUY AS A GIFT

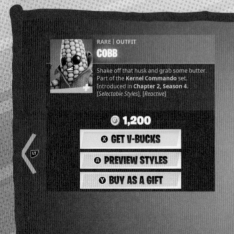

RARE | OUTFIT
COBB
Shake off that husk and grab some butter.
Part of the **Kernel Commando** set.
Introduced in **Chapter 2, Season 4**.
[Selectable Styles], [Reactive]

1,200

GET V-BUCKS
PREVIEW STYLES
BUY AS A GIFT

750

1 of 4

Corn pops with damage!

COBB

Classification: Rare
Price: 1,200

Cobb is the ideal choice of skin if you want to take a food theme into battle, but you're a vegetarian! Cobb is the result of a failed experiment, but the weirdest thing about him is that he likes to eat corn – making him both a vegetarian and a cannibal at the same time...

SKINS

BIG CHUGGUS

Classification: Slurp Series
Price: 1,500

Big Chuggus is, as you'd expect from the name, a pretty hefty skin. His bulging muscles and ripped physique are helped no doubt by the slurp juice coursing through his veins, the supply system for which is part of his armour.

BIG CHUGGUS
Small chugguses need not apply.
Part of the **Slurp Squad** set.
Introduced in **Chapter 2, Season 1**.

1,500
GET V-BUCKS
BUY AS A GIFT

DEADEYE
Bounty hunter from beyond the grave.
Part of the **Dark Visions** set.
Introduced in **Chapter 2, Season 1**.
[Selectable Styles]

2,000
GET V-BUCKS
PREVIEW STYLES

DEADEYE

Classification: Legendary
Price: 2,000

The spooky, spectral Deadeye is the spirit of a dead bounty hunter. With his glowing eyes and dark look, he's a great choice if you're looking to scare the life out of your rivals before you eliminate them...

SPARKPLUG

Classification: Rare
Price: 1,200

This master mechanic is often found on the island, offering to repair vehicles for a fee. She's forgotten more about car repairs than most people ever know – and now you can play as her too!

SPARKPLUG
Scrap the competition.
Part of the **Boneyard** set.
Introduced in **Season 7**.

1,200
PURCHASE ITEMS
BUY AS A GIFT

MECHA TEAM LEADER
Some assembly required.
Part of the **Final Showdown** set.
Introduced in **Season 9**.
[Built-in], [Selectable Styles]

1,600
GET V-BUCKS
PREVIEW STYLES

MECHA TEAM LEADER

Classification: Epic
Price: 1,600

The Mecha Team Leader is a throwback to Season 9 and played a big part in the Final Showdown live event. It's an amalgamation of various mech parts, topped off with a cuddly pink head. However, he isn't remotely cute so don't be fooled!

MUSIC, FILM AND YOUTUBER SKINS!

If you're excited about your 15 minutes of fame, why not skin up in one of these fantastic skins inspired by your favourite music, movies and YouTubers!

DJ BOPP

Classification: Legendary
Price: 2,000

DJ Bopp is the DJ that always brings the party. The outfit was first released way back in Season 7 and is the female version of DJ Yonder – but Bopp proved far more popular with fans than Yonder, and makes regular appearances in the game and Item Shop.

MAJOR LAZER

Classification: Icon
Price: 1,600

This skin was first introduced in Season X to celebrate a performance by Diplo, who is part of the group known as Major Lazer. It even comes with its own built-in emote – the Lazer Flex.

TRAVIS SCOTT

Classification: Icon
Price: 1,500

Travis Scott delivered a huge live concert in Fortnite back in Chapter 2 Season 2, entitled Astronomical. This skin was released to celebrate the event, and is a very popular one even now.

ASTRO JACK

Classification: Icon
Price: 2,000

Another part of the series celebrating Travis Scott's appearance in the game, Astro Jack is a reactive skin. He'll light up when bumped into, damaged by a weapon, or if there's music playing nearby – his face lights up!

THEGREFG

Classification: Icon
Price: 1,800

This skin pays tribute to the YouTuber who is a Fortnite legend in his own right. His Twitch channel has attracted over 2.4million users at the same time to watch him play Fortnite, so Epic recognized his legendary status with his very own skin!

ELLEN RIPLEY

Classification: Epic
Price: 1,500

Ripley is one of the bravest people in the universe, and if she can survive facehuggers in the airvents deep in space (where no-one can hear you scream) then a few opponents on the island should be easy!

HARLEY QUINN

Classification: DC Series
Price: 2,000

The unmistakable Harley Quinn is probably the coolest of the many DC characters that have made their way to Fortnite. Replicated in perfect detail, she's the perfect choice for any Fortnite gamer looking to spread a little craziness on the island.

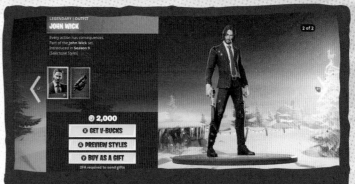

JOHN WICK

Classification: Legendary
Price: 2,000

John Wick eventually got his own skin in the game after an earlier skin, called The Reaper, bore such a strong resemblance to him that everyone called it John Wick anyway. This one's official – just don't hurt his dog.

REY

Classification: Star Wars Series
Price: 1,500

The last Jedi made it to Fortnite as part of the Star Wars tie-in that was so popular back in Chapter 2 Season 1. Part of a set called The New Trilogy, she's present here in the white robes we all associate with her from the films.

IMPERIAL STORMTROOPER

Classification: Star Wars Series
Price: 1,500

Is this the skin you're looking for? The Imperial Stormtrooper was another part of the Star Wars crossover and proved immediately successful. There's something pretty awesome about playing squads where you all use this skin – it certainly panics your opponents!

ANIMAL SKINS!

The island is teeming with wildlife, but that doesn't mean you only get to look at it. With this fantastic selection of skins you can get a little wild yourself!

FENNIX

Classification: Rare
Price: 1,200

This fabulously foxy fella was first released in Season X. A red and white fox, he comes fully dressed in battle armour, while those glowing orange eyes make him stand out even further.

RARE | OUTFIT
FENNIX
Never outfoxed.
Part of the **Fur Force** set.
Introduced in **Season X**.

1,200
PURCHASE ITEMS
BUY AS A GIFT

RARE | OUTFIT
HEARTBREAKER
Roses are red, violets are blue, victory is sweet, but not without you.
Part of the **Royale Hearts** set.
Introduced in **Season 7**.

1,200
PURCHASE ITEMS
BUY AS A GIFT

HEARTBREAKER

Classification: Rare
Price: 1,200

Certainly one of the more bonkers skins in Fortnite, this skin features a red llama covered in love hearts. Forget about trying to blend into the background – this skin is for gamers who are happy to be seen!

BIGFOOT

Classification: Rare
Price: 1,200

This legendary creature joined the Fortnite universe in Chapter 1 Season 9. The subject of decades of rumour and disputed sightings, he seems to have got over his shyness and is now only too happy to grab a shotgun and draw attention to himself...

RARE | OUTFIT
BIGFOOT
International man of mystery.
Part of the **Bigfoot** set.
Introduced in **Season 9**.

1,200
PURCHASE ITEMS
BUY AS A GIFT

| OUTFIT
TENDER DEFENDER
Protect your nuggets.
Part of the **Fowl Play** set.
Introduced in **Season 6**.

1,500
GET V-BUCKS
BUY AS A GIFT

TENDER DEFENDER

Classification: Epic
Price: 1,500

The Tender Defender is certainly no chicken when it comes to taking out opponents – but it is a chicken in pretty much every other way. It's fun to hang around the farm in this outfit and really confuse anyone that runs into you.

LEVIATHAN

Classification: Legendary
Price: 2,000

One of Fortnite's older skins, this unique-looking outfit first appeared way back in Season 3. The skin itself is just a suit, which is controlled by the fish floating freely in the helmet!

DARK TRICERA OPS

Classification: Dark Series
Price: 1,200

The female contemporary to Dark Rex, Dark Tricera Ops is a darker version of the original outfit and also has two styles – white and purple. It dates from Chapter 2 Season 1 and is a popular outfit that seems to only become available very occasionally.

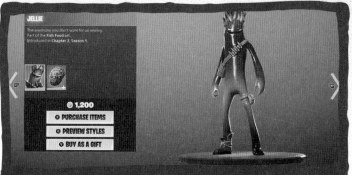

JELLIE

Classification: Rare
Price: 1,200

Jellie joined the Fortnite universe at the start of Chapter 2 Season 3, when Meowscles accidentally took him from his home while skiing. He appears to consist of slurp juice and glows brightly in the dark, as well as looking very distinctive.

DARK REX

Classification: Dark Series
Price: 1,200

This dino-tastic skin is hugely popular and has two styles- white and purple. Both are modeled on Jonesy, with the dinosaur head actually being a helmet that sits over the skin

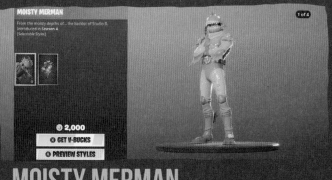

MOISTY MERMAN

Classification: Legendary
Price: 2,000

Another long-serving Fortnite skin, Moisty Merman is actually based on the monster from the 1954 classic film 'Creature from the Black Lagoon.' With his scaly skin and affinity for water, he blends in nicely to the sea if you fancy suprising land-based enemies from the water!

GROWLER

Classification: Epic
Price: 1,500

He may take the form of a dog, but don't be fooled – Growler is not the kind of animal you want to stroke in a hurry. If you do, you might lose a hand – look at those teeth!

SPORTS STARS

When they aren't engaging in a 100-1 battle to be the sole survivor, the residents of the island love their sport. Whatever it is you're into, there's a sporting outfit for you to wear while you're racking up the eliminations. Here are some of our favourites!

SPIKE

Classification: Epic
Price: 1,500

Spike is a heavily custimisable outfit, enabling you to add a number from 1-99 on his back and change lots of elements of his outfit so you can recreate your own favourite gridiron team to play as!

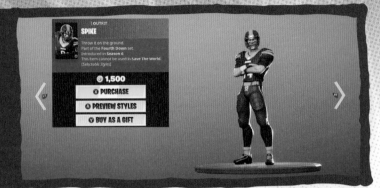

SURF RIDER

Classification: Rare
Price: 1,200

Surfrider is a wetsuit-clad surfer chick with a steely glint in her eye. She's a competitive boat racer, so the perfect choice if you like to spend a lot of your time causing mayhem from the boats dotted around the island!

BIRDIE

Classification: Uncommon
Price: 800

The calmness and serenity of the golf course is a million miles away from the action-packed goings-on in fortnite, but none of that seems to faze Birdie. This female golf character always performs above par.

WHISTLE WARRIOR

Classification: Uncommon
Price: 800

Another gridiron-based skin, Whistle Warrior is a female referee outfit. At only 800 V-Bucks she's a good bargain too – and what better way to settle disputes between fellow players than by eliminating them both?

FASTBALL

Classification: Rare
Price: 1,200

If baseball is your thing, then Fastball could be the skin for you! A baseball pitcher, she is as accurate with an assault rifle as she presumably is with a tiny leather ball.

ALPINE ACE

Classification: Epic
Price: 1,500

With so much of the island given over to mountainous terrain, Alpine Ace will feel right at home in Fortnite. There are seven different variations on this skin, and they are each individual rather than styles, so when it does pop up in the shop, make sure you select the one you want!

SLUGGER

Classification: Rare
Price: 1,200

Presumably Slugger is the mortal enemy of Fastball. This baseball big hitter comes complete with body armour, a helmet (safety first don't you know) and facepaint that actually helps him to stay concealed.

PAR PATROLLER

Classification: Uncommon
Price: 800

If this outfit looks familiar, it's because she is a summer version of Birdie. You'll only find her available during the warmer months of the year – which, lets face it, is the only sensible time to be spending hours on a golf course anyway, surely?

MATCH POINT

Classification: Uncommon
Price: 800

The only thing this tennis player is serving up is total destruction! Another summery outfit that looks sweetness and light when the truth is actually anything but!

MOGUL MASTER

Classification: Epic
Price: 1,500

Mogul Master is the female equivalent of Alpine ace. Like Alpine Ace, there are seven different variations, with each one being a different outfit rather than a selectable style – so be sure to choose carefully when making a purchase!

DYNAMO

Classification: Rare
Price: 1,200

Everyone loves wrestling, and Dynamo brings the glitz, glamour and downright craziness of the sport to the island. Her face mask and lycra make for an interesting option, but again – hiding in the undergrowth isn't easy when dressed like this!

CHAPTER 2 SEASON 7 SKINS

Here are some of the newest skins that only landed during Chapter 2 Season 7! Many are new looks for returning favourites, but if you want to let people know how much you love Fortnite, there's no better way to do it than by strutting around in the latest skins?

MIDSUMMER MIDAS

Classification: Epic
Price: 1,600

We all thought Midas was done for when he appeared to be eaten by a shark at the end of Chapter 2 Season 2, but perhaps the shark couldn't digest solid gold? In any case, Midas is back in this relaxed summer outfit.

BOARDWALK RUBY

Classification: Rare
Price: 1,200

Another Fortnite old-timer, Ruby has been around since Season X, and has appeared in a couple of different variations since. Her boardwalk look is new for Chapter 2 Season 7, meaning she fits in well with Believer Beach's party vibe.

BEACH JULES

Classification: Rare
Price: 1,200

Jules is Midas' daughter. Not content with living in his shadow, she has developed a ruthless reputation all of her own – and now you can take her to the beach. Even international criminals need to unwind, after all.

BEACH BRUTUS

Classification: Rare
Price: 1,200

Brutus is a gangster who is out for himself, and he worked for both Ghost and Shadow – but his real loyalty was only ever to himself. However, being a double agent is tiring, so he's slipped his shorts on and headed for the beach.

BEACH BOMBER

Classification: Rare
Price: 1,200

Beach Bomber was first released way back in Season 9, and often returns during summer party events. Her bright rainbow T-shirt makes her stick out like a sore thumb though – not one to use if you like a spot of stealth!

PARTY MVP

Classification: Epic
Price: 1,500

A bright, skintight outfit and blue or pink hair as a selectable option? Two things are certain here. One – you'll look fabulous. Two – you can forget about hiding in the darkness!

NIGHTLIFE

Classification: Epic
Price: 1,500

This outfit looks good enough to start with, but the reason this is one of our favourite features is that this is a reactive outfit. When Nitelife is near music, her suit will light up and change pattern. It might give away your position but who cares when you look this cool?

LITESHOW

Classification: Uncommon
Price: 800

Weighing in at just 800 V-Bucks, this skin is a bargain way to look ready to party. Liteshow's neon pattern glows brightly in the dark, so you'll always be ready to get your groove on!

GET YOUR GROOVE ON!

ONE OF THE MANY THINGS ABOUT FORTNITE THAT REALLY MAKE IT STANDS OUT FROM MORE SERIOUS GAMES IN THE GENRE IS THE TONGUE-IN-CHEEK GENIUS THAT IS THE DANCE EMOTES. FOR MANY YEARS IT'S BEEN A TRADITION IN MULTIPLAYER TO MOCK VANQUISHED OPPONENTS, BUT WITHOUT AN IN-GAME WAY OF DOING SO, THE ONLY OPTIONS TENDED TO BE QUITE AGGRESSIVE – REPEATEDLY CROUCHING OVER A FALLEN OPPONENT IN HALO, FOR EXAMPLE.

Fortnite changed all that overnight by introducing dance moves into the game itself, meaning you can now show off with an impromptu boogie that may well be rubbing your opponent's nose in it a little – but is almost guaranteed to bring a smile to their lips as well.

It was a masterstroke. By effectively nerfing 'in your face' celebrations, Epic helped make Fortnite feel like a friendlier place than most other shooters – and the dances caught on quickly too!

Chelsea Lauren/Shutterstock

Gilles Mingasson/ABC/Shutterstock

THE FLOSS

Perhaps the most famous of all the Fortnite dances, the Floss has been the source of some controversy. The Backpack Kid, a famous Instagram dancer, made it famous when he performed it on Saturday Night Live in 2017, accompanying Katy Perry's song Swish Swish. It appeared in Fortnite shortly afterwards and since then, the legal battle about who owns the dance has run and run! It's also been performed by Dele Alli, the Tottenham footballer, while Millie Bobbie Brown from Stranger Things has also posted videos of her doing it too!

FRESH

The dance performed by Carlton from the Fresh Prince of Bel Air is an absolute classic – even though many Fortnite players will be far too young to have seen the series first time round. The song he always performs it to is 'Not Unusual' by Tom Jones, and this was a hugely popular addition to the Fortnite dance world!

RIDE THE PONY

This is another dance sensation that had swept the world before arriving in Fortnite. Gangnam style was a viral hit by South Korean rapper Psy. The song mocks the rich people who live in the Gangnam area of Seoul (or, more specifically, wannabes who pretend that they are posh). The dance pokes fun at them all claiming to own ponies and horses – and it is a cracker!

Lee Jin-Man/AP/Shutterstock

SAY SO

Another very firm favourite from TikTok, this dance quickly sprang up as a viral accompaniment to Doja Cat's song of the same name! Before long, millions of people all over the world were posting themselves performing it, and Fortnite players wanted in on the action!

BLINDING LIGHT

The dance to accompany the Weeknd's song Blinding Lights originated on TikTok and became a huge viral challenge. You know what that means! It popped up in Fortnite quick smart, priced at 500 VBucks!

PLEASE DON'T STOP THE MUSIC

A LOOK AT THE MUSIC THAT'S PROVIDING THE BACKING TRACK TO OUR FAVOURITE GAME!

connect with people who might not listen to their music otherwise, making new fans along the way.

The big musical events in Fortnite have certainly achieved that for the artists involved. The first concert to take place in the main game itself was by Marshmello in 2019 and, at the time, it was the biggest in-game event ever. According to Epic, 10.7 million people were in the game at the time of the concert, with millions more watching via live streams on Twitch. The official recap video of the concert has almost sixty million views on YouTube at the time of going to press – further proof that the audience for music in Fortnite is absolutely huge.

❚❚ THE GIG, WHICH WAS ENTITLED ASTRONOMICAL, LASTED JUST 15 MINUTES BUT TOOK IN BITS OF SOME OF SCOTT'S BIGGEST HITS INCLUDING 'GOOSEBUMPS', 'SICKO MODE', AND 'HIGHEST IN THE ROOM ❚❚

As any Fortnite fan knows, Epic has created much more than a game. At its very heart, Fortnite is a community, a cultural reference point we can all share. With the launch of Party Royale in May 2020, you don't even have to play the game in order to join in the fun – there's now a space where you can hang with your friends, meet new people, and even listen to music.

Music has always been a big part of Fortnite, but over the last couple of years, Epic has gone all out to make it an even more central part of what you can expect from the game. In some ways, the lack of live music during the Covid-19 pandemic made the possibility of an appearance in Fortnite an even more appealing prospect for artists. At a time when touring became impossible and we all started to find different ways to engage with our musical heroes, it isn't hard to see why playing a virtual gig makes complete sense.

What's more, appearing in a game like Fortnite brings wider exposure for artists, giving them the chance to

Even those huge figures were dwarfed the following year when Travis Scott took to the Fortnite stage as an in-game event. This time, over 12 million people were in the game to witness the concert live. The gig, which was entitled Astronomical, lasted just 15 minutes but took in bits of some of Scott's biggest hits including 'Goosebumps', 'Sicko Mode', and 'Highest in the Room'. All three titles re-entered Spotify's top ten in the US after the event!

Such mega events are certainly popular, but they take a lot of planning and organising and can't be too regular in the main game without losing their appeal. However, Epic has made it clear that they want musical artists to become a regular feature of the Fortnite world, albeit in a smaller way than megastars like Travis Scott and Marshmello.

❚❚ IT'S A UNIQUE WAY TO REACH AN AUDIENCE THAT MAYBE YOU'RE NOT REACHING THROUGH OTHER MEANS ❚❚

Nate Nanzer, Fortnite's Head of Global Partnership, has described Fortnite as a 'tour stop' for bands and musicians. 'If you're on tour, you want to stop on the Fortnite stage,' he said in 2020. 'It's a unique way to reach an audience that maybe you're not reaching through other means.

Party Royale is certainly a great step in that direction. The game environment is home to a concert stage and an outdoor cinema, and Epic is working hard to make sure both are used as often as possible. Because Party Royale does not feature weapons and is just a place where people can meet up, talk and party, it's much easier for Epic to incorporate music events into the game.

Artists including Diplo (as Major Lazer), Steve Aoki, Deadmau5 and Kenshi Yonezu were amongst the first to perform on the music stage in Party Royale, but for the most part these were very basic attempts at bringing a concert experience to Fortnite. They all relied on nothing more complicated than the DJ performing at home and the music being beamed into the game – nothing too fancy or immersive there. But Epic is determined to change that, and has promised a new series of concerts that will change the way the world thinks about 'virtual gigs'.

It's a responsibility that the company has taken seriously. A new studio has been constructed in Los Angeles that features state of the art technology that will enable artists to be filmed and recorded so that they appear in the game 'live' when they perform their gigs. It's been designed so it can even be operated remotely in case there are any more Covid-19 restrictions brought in, meaning that the music can continue uninterrupted in the world of Fortnite whatever is happening in the real world.

The concert series – which Epic is calling Spotlight - began with three performances by hip-hop artist Dominic Fike in September 2020. He was joined in Epic's studio by his backing band as he performed a number of tracks from his debut album What Could Possibly Go Wrong.

It was a huge success, and Epic followed it up shortly afterwards with another Spotlight performance by Anderson .Paak, with the show repeated twice to make sure different time zones didn't miss out.

It's an interesting new approach to seeing live music, and one that Epic is clearly very committed to in the future – building a new recording studio won't have been cheap, and neither is paying the artists to perform. Rumour has it that Travis Scott picked up somewhere around $20 million for his live gig, so expect to see many more artists making their way to the Fortnite stage over the course of 2022!

MOVIE MAGIC

It's not just music that we're seeing more of in Party Royale! The open-air cinema has been used to show a number of Christopher Nolan films, including Inception, Batman Begins and the Prestige. It's also been used to show a trailer for Tenet (no, we've got no idea what happened in the movie either, so don't write in...) as well as Nineteen Eighty-Fortnite, Epic's short film criticising Apple for banning Fortnite from its devices.

RADIO GAGA

As well as the live concerts and events in the game, you can also listen to music on the radios in the vehicles in the game. The various radio stations have featured loads of different songs, including Sunflower by Post Malone and Swae Lee, Don't Start Now by Dua Lipa, and I Don't Care by Ed Sheeran & Justin Bieber. The playlist changes often so it stays on trend!

STAY TUNED ON SOCIAL MEDIA!

If you like the growing influence that music is having on fortnite, then you can delve into more of it on social media. Spotify is home to a playlist called Fortnite Radio Tracks that features every song that's played on the in-game radio stations – and more are added whenever the playlist updates!

There are also plenty of other fortnite-themed playlists on there, many curated by fans and YouTubers that include the in-game music too!

If you want to see the official videos of the gigs by TravisScott and Marshmello, you can find them on YouTube. Search for 'Travis Scott and Fortnite Present: Astronomical (Full Event Video)' and 'Marshmello Holds First Ever Fortnite Concert Live At Pleasant Park' to find the official video from each artist!

INSPIRED CREATIONS!

ONE OF THE COOL THINGS EPIC CHANGED IN CREATIVE MODE WAS MAKING IT EASIER TO FIND MAPS BASED AROUND SIMILAR THEMES BY EXPLORING THE TABS ACROSS THE TOP OF THE 'DISCOVER' SECTION OF THE GAME.

We've hunted through thousands of user-created maps to find some great game ideas and maps grouped around your favourite themes – check them out!

STAR WARS

THE STAR WARS UNIVERSE HAS BEEN HOME TO SOME TRULY INCREDIBLE ADVENTURES – SO HERE ARE SOME FANTASTIC STAR WARS SETTINGS FOR YOU TO TAKE YOUR PARTY ONLINE WITH!

STAR WARS DESTROYER HIDE AND SEEK

Created by: Makamakes
Island code: 8794-6005-7458

From the map-making legend Makamakes comes this great map, ideal for the hide and seek game that it is host to. The sprawling enormity of a Galactic Empire Destroyer is captured brilliantly, with everything from Stormtrooper quarters to huge hangars that are home to TIE fighters.

The game itself is simple – two hiders and sixteen seekers are unleashed onto the Destroyer, so sneaking around and keeping quiet is the order of the day!

Watch out the seekers are coming!

BATTLE OF ENDOR

Created by: The Windos **Island code:** 5320-5459-5518

This faithful recreation of the Battle of Endor has everything you'd hope for, from the Imperial Shuttle docked at the start of the level to the thick undergrowth and vegetation of Endor itself.

Looking up, you'll find the wooden walkways that the Ewoks employed to such great effect are all present and correct, while some clever thinking from creator The Windos means that a large part of the map is set inside the underground corridors of an Empire outpost, providing an interesting variety to the greenery and open spaces outside.

ROGUE ONE BATTLE FOR SCARIF

Created by: ProSpartaner **Island code:** 7122-7510-1638

One of the real standout moments from Rogue One: A Star Wars Story was the incredible Battle for Scarif scene, where a small rebel force tried to gain access to the servers holding the plans for the Death Star.

The battle was intense, set on an amazing island, and this map captures every detail absolutely brilliantly. The action is frozen in time as AT-ATs, X-Wings and TIE Fighters do battle all around you, leaving you to concentrate on a 16-player Fortnite battle!

BATTLE FOR HOTH

Created by: Enderbite **Island code:** 1105-0474-2463

Time for some Empire Strikes Back nostalgia now, with this fantastic map set on the ice planet of Hoth. In the film, this was home to the iconic battle between the Snow Speeders and AT-ATs with the speeders bringing down their hulking opponents using cunning rather than force.

This map allows two teams to do battle, with loadouts assigned based on the different roles on each side that you can assume. It captures the spirit of Hoth perfectly and makes for a great backdrop for a battle with your fellow party members!

MARVEL AVENGERS

THE AVENGERS HAVE BEEN AN ESSENTIAL PART OF THE FORTNITE UNIVERSE FOR SOME TIME NOW, AND THERE ARE SOME FANTASTIC MAPS AND GAME STYLES YOU CAN ENJOY. HERE ARE JUST A HANDFUL OF OUR FAVOURITES!

AVENGERS TOWER

Created by: earth_official **Island Code:** 2023-3582-0967

This sprawling map features the Avengers Tower at its very heart, complete with helipad! The surrounding streets are all fair game as the combat unfolds. The attention to detail from earth_official is really impressive as anyone who has seen any of the Avengers movies will know – even the surrounding streets look authentic.

Kit up in Avengers gear and head onto this map for some serious fun!

HELICARRIER – SUPERHERO ARENA

Created by: MakaMakes
Island Code: 8058-5258-8241

This is another amazing map from MakaMakes, cementing his reputation as a Fortnite Creative giant. A highly detailed recreation of the SHIELD helicarrier, the bit that will really blow your mind is knowing that this map was initially built in just four hours for a YouTube challenge!

It's all here, from the craft on the carrier itself to the bridge area that's been in so many Avengers movie scenes. There's also fun to be had because the map features the open areas of the deck as well as the tight corridors below decks to give you the best of both worlds – and of course, as it is suspended in the air there's no running away so the battle will be fast and furious!

WELCOME TO ASGARD!

Created by: nooEl-gaming
Island Code: 0513-4644-9670

Prepare to have thy jaw drop, mere mortal! This stunning recreation of Thor's home city of Asgard boasts incredible attention to detail – it looks exactly like the shots from the movies. It's all here, from Odin's Vault to Biofrost, the rainbow bridge linking Asgard to Midgard.

Suit up as Thor and his avengers pals to really make the most out of exploring against this glorious backdrop which is a testament to what can be achieved by the incredibly talented creative community can achieve in Fortnite.

TYCOON GAMES

REMEMBER CLASSIC BUILDING GAMES LIKE ROLLERCOASTER TYCOON? WELL, THE TALENTED CREATIVE COMMUNITY HAS TAKEN THAT IDEA AND INCORPORATED IT INTO FORTNITE GAMES!

MARS TYCOON

Created by: Brendannd
Island Code: 9970-8799-7074

The premise for this game is that you have been stranded on Mars and must escape the hostile planet as quickly as possible. Think of it as like the film The Martian, only you're in a race against other players to escape.

You begin with your own base and need to collect gold so that you can purchase farmbots that can grow more gold for your needs. The more gold you have, the more things you can access. You can unlock robot guards to keep your base safe from attackers, for example, while you try and launch raids on other bases to damage your rivals' chances.

Most important is unlocking the rocket base, which will enable you to escape Mars to safety – but the challenge is to get enough resources ahead of your opponents to do so!

LIFE SIMULATOR

Created by: FCT_-
Island Code: 3037-5973-1417

If you like The Sims almost as much as you like Fortnite, then this is the game mode for you! You need to keep your Fortnite character happy by paying close attention to the four mood bars – Hunger, Energy, Social and Fun. Just like in The Sims these will all deplete over time so you need to perform actions that will give them a boost every so often.

Career-wise, you have different skills to work on – Charisma, Intelligence, Creativity and Strength. The more you work on these and the higher your stats, the better your chances of being promoted. All that's left to do is choose a career path from working in a gym, library, internet café, laboratory, or as a Love Ranger!

VEHICLE-BASED GAMES

THE DIFFERENT VEHICLES IN FORTNITE ARE HUGELY POPULAR, SO IT'S INEVITABLE THAT SOME PLAYERS HAVE CREATED ENTIRE GAMES BASED ON DRIVING, SAILING AND FLYING. HERE ARE SOME OF THE VERY BEST GAMES USING VEHICLES AS A KEY PART OF THE GAMEPLAY!

Drive To ORANGE!

COLOR DASH

Created by: MrMonkeyFN
Island Code: 0321-8998-8494

The premise behind this game is simple – you'll be placed onto a map consisting of coloured tiles. Then all the players will be told which colour they need to drive to in order to be safe. Your task is to drive to the colour selected as quickly as you can, because all the other tiles will disappear and anyone on them will be eliminated.

Of course, this is Fortnite so you can boost your chances of success a little by deliberately ramming your opponents to slow them down, or even knocking them off the tile if they end up on the same one as you!

RUNNERS VS CARS

Created by: Axel-Capek **Island Code:** 5287-5167-4148

This game mode is absolute mayhem and you can play either in the vehicles or as a parkour player. If you're driving a vehicle the aim is to take out the runners, while if you are on foot, you must run the gauntlet and destroy the object at the end that the cars are trying to protect.

It's a fast and furious experience that helps you master lots of techniques that will be useful in Battle Royales!

CHOPPA RACERS

Created by: Choupala
Island Code: 4053-4576-7391

If you want to master the art of flying, then this is the game for you. You take control of a choppa and must navigate your way through 15 gates in a futuristic setting. Making it through each one safely becomes successively harder as the game goes on, with the clock ticking as you race to beat either your own best time, or the other members of your party in the race!

ZIGZAGZONG CAR RACE **Created by:** Zigi **Island Code:** 3417-5493-5083

This car race level is not so much about speed but close control of your vehicle. It is packed full of twists and turns, with very few opportunities to put your foot down and get some speed behind you instead, you'll be using the handbrake to slide round tight corners and dodging past awkwardly placed obstacles. Smart use of the boost button can help you climb some of the fiendish ramps but look out – you'll still be running into obstacles at regular intervals.

CLIMBERS VS DRIVERS: AVALANCHE

Created by: KKSlider **Island Code:** 7999-1041-1393

This takes a pretty traditional game mode in Fortnite creative – avalanche – and adds a whole new element in the form of cars. You'll assume either the role of a climber or a driver. The climbers are trying to reach the top of the mountain as per usual in avalanche game types, but the twist this time round is that you can also play as a car driver, hurtling down the mountain and wiping out the climbers as you go!

UPTOWN ROAD RUSH

Created by: Vojj47 **Island Code:** 9833-1277-9143

This is a great zombie-chasing mode that sees you dropped into a small town over-run by the undead. Your mission is simple enough – to drive round it, running over as many zombies as you can. You can leave your vehicle if you want to grab weapons and deal damage on foot, but be warned – you'll find yourself overwhelmed by zombies pretty quickly if you do!

THE BEST CREATORS

ONE OF THE REALLY COOL THINGS ABOUT FORTNITE (OKAY OKAY, THERE ARE LOTS OF COOL THINGS ABOUT FORTNITE!) IS THE WAY THAT CREATIVE MODE ALLOWS TALENTED FANS TO ACTUALLY CREATE THEIR OWN GAMES, GAME TYPES AND MAPS.

Inevitably, there are some truly talented creatives out there who constantly deliver maps and games that are every bit as good as the ideas that Epic themselves come up with. **We take a look at some of the creative content to keep an eye out for from the biggest names on the scene!**

FINEST

TWITTER: @FN _ FINEST
YOUTUBE: FINEST

FINEST IS A VERY POPULAR MAP CREATOR WHEN IT COMES TO SMALL-SIDED, REALISTIC GAMES OF FORTNITE, GIVING YOU THE CHANCE TO PRACTICE YOUR BUILDING SKILLS TO HELP YOU IN THOSE BUILD BATTLES IN BATTLE ROYALES

FINEST REALISTIC (2X2)

Island Code: 6570-5231-1418

This is a small island map, like so many of Finest's creations. You'll start just a few yards from your opponents carrying a decent paylod – this will vay based on what players vote for in the pre-match lobby, with set rules making the decision in the event of a tie.

You'll also start with lots of materials, and the building is pretty instantaneous. It's a fantastic way to learn how to build quickly, because there's little other option! The game starts small and the storm moves in quickly so you'll be on top of each other from the start – often literally! There is a small hut on the map which you can use to build on or around, but it is usually consumed by the player-crested buildings pretty quickly!

FINEST REALISTIC (1V1-4V4V4V4)

Island code: 6078-7811-0032

This map can work with as few as 1v1 or as as many as four squads involved. Again, you can settle on a payload vote in the pre-match lobby, and will start with plenty of materials. The map features a cliff face leading down to a beach, with lots of water featuring – the centre of the storm circle is actually over the water so you'll certainly need to build in the latter stages, even if you can get away without doing so to start with.

WINTER SPORTS ZONE WARS

Island Code: 9520-3293-4391

A little change of direction from Finest, here, who tends to focus on small, realistic, build-intensive maps. This downhill winter-sports-themed effort makes life interesting because the zone is always moving until it reaches a final strom circle. While you can still build, the storm will move to consume whatever has been constructed until it reaches the final circle, at which point it will shrink as normal.

It makes for a game where building, firing, then quickly moving on are key elements of the gameplay – there's certainly no time to waste by bushcamping or hiding, but the ever-moving nature of the map does make for some interesting experiences.

ENIGMA

WHEN IT COMES TO A VARIETY OF MAPS AND GAME TYPES, LOOK NO FURTHER THAN ENGIMA, WHO CREATES EVERYTHING FROM TINY 1V1 BOX WARS TO GIANT SPRAWLING TEAM DEATH MATCHES! ENIGMA'S ATTENTION TO DETAIL IS INCREDIBLE – LOTS OF THESE MAPS WOULD NOT LOOK OUT OF PLACE IN THE GAME ITSELF.

HEADSHOTS ONLY PUMP WARS (BOX FIGHT)

Island Code: 0545-1862-6292

This is a great enclosed map that takes place in a large room. It's designed to increase your shotgun accuracy, encouraging players to build structures as they try to out-manoeuver each other and get close enough to land a headshot with the shotgun. Only headshots will count, nothing else, so you will find you improve both your building and your shotgun skills on this map. If you find it too hard and are dying too much, the game has an inbuilt handicap system that will give you extra health to help you last a little longer while you get the hang of things!

COLD FRONT (SURVIVAL) Island Code: 5791-4774-9462

This exciting game mode starts on a plane that has crashed in the Antarctic. Your mission is to survive at all costs, taking care of your needs for hunger, thirst and warmth.

That means you need to catch fish to eat, build wells to drink, and light fires to keep warm. It's a totally different gaming experience to Fortnite and very well implemented. Of course, Enigma has made things even harder with the inclusion of ice zombies that attack you at regular intervals. The game becomes a battle to build a base from where you can make excursions to gather the resources you need to stay alive. It's great fun and highly recommended for a very different take on Fortnite!

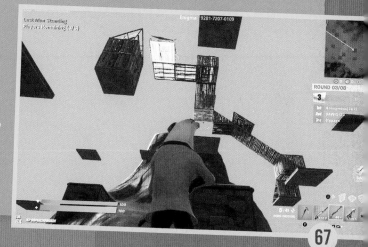

50 PLAYER PERFORMANCE (ZONE WAR)

Island Code: 2643-2398-4554

Get READY TO RUMBLE! This is a massive zone war, where the circle shifts location throughout the game. With a massive 50 players involved, this makes for carnage as you are all always pretty close to your rivals in the game The storm moves you all so that you are forced to head up a mountain side, meaning you'll need to be confident both building and fighting under pressure at speed. It's fast and furious, that's for sure!

PANDVIL

TWITTER: @PANDVIL
YOUTUBE: PANDVIL

PANDVIL IS ANOTHER SOLID MAP MAKER WHO IS AS COMFORTABLE CREATING SMALL ARENA BATTLES AS LARGE, SPRAWLING EFFORTS.

PANDVIL BOX FIGHTS (2V2 FILL)

Island Code: 6562-8953-6567

Set inside a tiny confined space, this is a 2x2 fill mode that's an absolute blast! You'll need to be building quickly from the very start but be warned – you don't have far you can move. Mastering this map will all come down to building above and around your opponents before dropping down to finish them off.

3V3V3V3 GO GOATED! (ZONE WARS)

Island Code: 7285-8843-2762

This game sees players starting on one of four colour-coded containers, with a central station in the middle. You can buy items and weapons from inside your containers to tool up before heading out into a small combat zone, or just go hell for leather and make a run for the centre. If you can make it to the middle and survive long enough, you'll become a pilot, reappearing in a plane and able to wreak havoc on the other players down below!

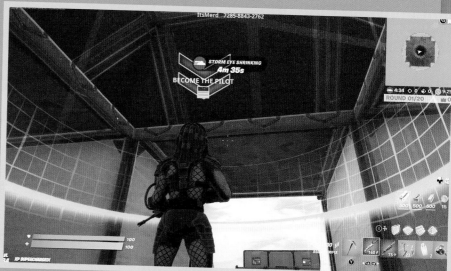

REALISTIC PVP (FREE FOR ALL)

Island Code: 0563-9687-6084

This a brilliantly designed island, based round a central valley with sea on one side and land on the other. The middle often becomes home to build battles, but there is enough wooded terrain round the outside of the map to play the map however you want to. The action is pretty hectic but there's plenty of goodies to pick up and it really does feel that the map never plays out the same way twice.

3D LAB

TWITTER: **@3DLABFN**

YOUTUBE: **3D LAB – FORTNITE CREATIVE**

3D LAB IS ACTUALLY A COMBINATION OF THREE DIFFERENT MAP DESIGNERS WORKING TOGETHER. EACH IS AMAZING IN THEIR OWN RIGHT, BUT TOGETHER, THEY MAKE FOR AN UNSTOPPABLE FORCE. THE TEAM OF @AXELCAPEK, @TINYMANIAC AND @BERTSCREATIONS ARE RESPONSIBLE FOR SOME OUTSTANDING MAPS, SOME OF WHICH HAVE EVEN BEEN INSPIRED BY OTHER GAMES.

NUKETOWN 2077 (GUN GAME)

Island Code: 4199-8785-5901

This map is inspired by the Nuketown map from the Call of Duty series, given an update and projected into the future. You can play a number of different game modes on the map, including Free For All, Bounty Hunter and Last Man Standing. Players will vote for the game type in the lobby, and load-outs are random unless the chosen game mode specifies otherwise.

The action is based around the end of a closed street, with a number of buildings to hide in, all forming a semi-circle – so the next shot could come from anywhere!

TILTED TOWERS ROYAL + CHOPPAS (FREE FOR ALL)

Island Code: 4595-8390-2418

This is a faithful recreation of an old Fortnite Favourite – the original hot drop itself, Tilted Towers! The layout and buildings are all as you'd expect, but you can't build or deform the existing layout.

To make up for that though, the map does include choppas so you can fly around and see Tilted Towers from above for a rather different perspective.

TUMBLE LADS (RACING)

Island Code: 5361-9496-2479

A bright and colourful racing experience, this map challenges you to slip, slide, jump and run your way through a variety of gaudily-coloured obstacle courses as quickly as you can! There are a few different game modes within the races on offer.

It's an interesting and fun change to the norm, and will help you improve your mobility – a skill that might come in handy the next tme you are trying to outrun the storm!

MAKAMAKES

TWITTER: @MAKAMAKES
YOUTUBE: MAKAMAKES – FORTNITE

MAKAMAKES IS A LEGEND ON THE FORTNITE GAMING SCENE WHEN IT COMES TO INTRICATELY DETAILED MAPS. HIS ATTENTION TO DETAIL IS INCREDIBLE AND HE HAS BROUGHT SOME AMAZING SETTINGS TO THE FORTNITE WORLD – BOTH FROM THE REAL WORLD AND FILMS!

MINI BR (BATTLE ROYALE)

Island Code: 8566-1472-7195

This outstanding mini-map would not look out of place as a real location in the game. It's based around a harbour/lagoon area, with clean modern buildings and nicely manicured vegetation. The shape of the map, with long roads above water, make for exciting gameplay as the storm circle shrinks.

You'll feel like you are in somewhere like Dubai playing this map – the architecture is very consistent with that part of the world and, like all MakaMakes maps, everything has been well thought through and placed so that it really belongs as part of the map's architecture.

AIRPORT (EXPLORATION)

Island Code: 6037-9905-6392

MakaMakes' sprawling airport map is another jaw-dropping example of just what is possible in Fortnite Creative mode. Everything you'd expect to find in a real airport is here – from passport control to baggage reclaim, with even an arrivals lounge and a shopping mall thrown in for good measure.

Outside, you'll find two runways for planes to use while they land and take off, as well as a giant helicopter hangar. While you can't fly the planes or helicopters, you can board some of the planes to look around the interior. There's even a plane forever frozen at takeoff – wonder where it's off to?

CROKE PARK (FREE FOR ALL)

Island Code: 6236-6720-2528

Croke Park is a famous stadium in Dublin. It's traditionaly home to Gaelic sports such as Hurling and Gaelic football, but the Irish rugby team and football team have both also played matches there.

This map brings it to life in absolutely remarkable detail, against the backdrop of a free for all game mode.

TEAMUNITE

TWITTER: @TEAMUNITEFN
YOUTUBE: TEAM UNITE

TEAMUNITE IS ANOTHER TEAM EFFORT, CONSISTING OF TWO CREATIVE PLAYERS THAT WORK TOGETHER TO MAKE GREAT MAPS. BETWEEN THEM, ECHO BUILDS AND FN CREATIVE TUTOR, THE MEMBERS OF TEAMUNITE, ALSO PUBLISH REALLY GOOD ONLINE TUTORIALS TO HELP SHOW HOW THEY DO IT!

THE SLOPES (COIN RACE) Island Code: 7224-8139-0230

While modern games like Fortnite are our faves, of course, that doesn't mean we don't sometimes miss the old-school days of collecting rings as Sonic the Hedgehog or coins as Super Mario.

This game mode allows you to enjoy some old-fashioned platform gaming brilliance in the modern-day setting of Fortnite. You'll find yourself hurtling down a ski slope, needing to slide left and right to hit jumps and reach as many coins as you can by the time you hit the bottom!

COLOUR SWITCH (MINI GAME)

Island Code: 0387-1152-4745

It's always fun to try something little different and this minigame ticks that box perfectly. It's also a great way to test your reflexes! You'll find yourself standing on a large floor made up of different coloured tiles. A colour will appear on the screen, and you have just a few seconds to make sure you are standing on a tile of that colour. All the other tiles will then disappear, knocking you out of the game if you aren't on the right tile.

Over time, you are given less and less time to reach the coloured tiles – and to make things more difficult the floor is icy so you'll slide around a little bit too. You'll need to control your inertia to stop yourself sliding off your tile to your doom!

COLOUR DIVE

Island Code: 0237-4476-7608

This game mode will really help you hone your skydiving skills so you can nail your landings in the game! The premise is simple – you'll be skydiving through a sky full of coloured hoops. The game will tell you which coloured hoops to aim for and you must make it through that hoop or be eliminated. It sounds easy but it really isn't – the action gets steadily faster the longer you survive!

STAYING SAFE

FORTNITE IS A BRILLIANT GAME AS WE ALL KNOW, BUT IT IS STILL IMPORTANT THAT YOU KNOW HOW TO KEEP YOURSELF SAFE WHEN YOU PLAY ONLINE. HERE ARE OUR TOP TIPS FOR KEEPING FORTNITE A FUN-FILLED ZONE!

VOICE CHAT

You can talk to other gamers in your squad or on your team, but you might not always want to. There's no real need to play through a headset unless you are in a squad with your friends because you can communicate through the in-game system to suggest destinations, warn your team-mates about possible attacks and so on. You should only use your headset to talk to people you know – for the rest of the time, you really don't need the chat function enabled!

PAYMENT DETAILS

If you've linked a payment method to your account, it's really important that you keep this private. The safest ways to pay for things in fortnite are via PayPal or using a credit card (or the credit card of an adult that you can use with permission, if you aren't old enough for one yourself). This means that if anyone DOES hack your account, you'll be insured against any fraud – and with PayPal, they'll only be able to take however much you've uploaded.

DO NOT USE A DEBIT CARD TO PLAY ONLINE!
Look, we used shouty capitals and everything! If you do this and you get hacked, then the hacker could drain your account in the blink of an eye – and you won't get that money back from your bank!

DON'T SHARE LOG-IN DETAILS

One of the easiest ways scammers work in Fortnite is to offer to play using your account to unlock things for you. It can be really tempting if a good player messages you to say they'll do it for you – after all, it saves you time doesn't it? Don't fall for it. If you give someone else your password, they can use it to hack your account and steal money from you. They might try the same password on other accounts you have, too. Never EVER let anyone else have your password!

Only YOU can prevent V-Buck Scams
Do not share your password with anyone.

CTING.

IN FORTNITE

REPORT PLAYER

FEEDBACK TYPE   REASON

Offensive Language

Offensive Name

Ⓐ Harassment/Abusive Gameplay

Teaming up with Enemies

AFK/Non-participation

Ⓑ BACK

Ⓨ [P2] LOG IN (HOLD)

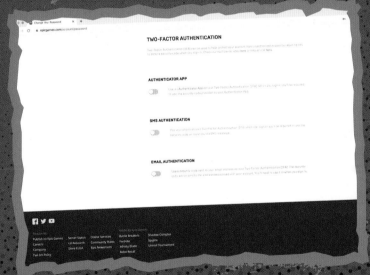

REPORT BAD BEHAVIOUR

Whatever format you play on, make sure you know how to use the settings to block, mute and report players who behave inappropriately. Epic can and does ban players who are found to be saying hateful things, but that's only possible if the rest of us report that behaviour.

You can report players directly to Epic from the menu, and give a reason why you are reporting them. You can also provide more information under the 'additional info' tab.

You can also report people to the online gaming service of whichever format you are playing on, and you should do this too if someone is using hate speech or behaving in a way that makes you feel uncomfortable. The specifics vary from each machine, but make sure you know how to report players, and do so if they behave inappropriately.

TWO-FACTOR AUTHENTICATION

Two Factor Authentication (or 2FA for short) is an easy way to keep your Fortnite account more secure. It means that whenever someone tries to access your Fortnite account from a new machine, you'll be asked to prove that it is you by entering a code that Fortnite will send to you. This can be sent to you by email or through an authenticator app, whichever is easiest for you – or, for extra safety, you can provide the details of your parent or guardian.

To register, all you need to do is visit www.fortnite.com/2FA. You even get a free emote – Boogie Down – just for registering. What's not to love?

CYBER BULLYING

If you are being bullied online, make sure you tell a parent or guardian or, if you don't feel able to talk to them, a teacher at school. No-one deserves to be bullied, whether it is online or otherwise, so make sure someone knows what is going on so they can help you to deal with it. Reporting bullies is a start, but sometimes it helps to talk to someone about the experience so we feel safer – and can get back to enjoying our gaming sessions!

You can also talk to charities like cybersmile.org or visit their website, which has lots of useful advice.

FORTNITE DICTIONARY

IF YOU'RE NEW TO FORTNITE (AND EVEN IF YOU'RE NOT!) A LOT OF THE LANGUAGE USED BY PLAYERS IN THE GAME CAN BE CONFUSING. THAT'S WHERE THIS LITTLE GUIDE COMES IN — ALL OF THE SLANG PHRASES USED BY FORTNITE GAMERS EXPLAINED SO YOU NEED NEVER LOOK LIKE A NOOB AGAIN!

WHAT THEY SAY	WHAT THEY MEAN
AR, regular AR	Normal Assault Rifle
Bandies	Bandages
Bots	A term for someone who isn't very good at the game and plays as if they are computer controlled
Box fight	When all the players in a battle start building themselves into boxes to protect themselves
Bubble	What some players call the storm circle – ie 'head to the bubble quickly, the storm is closing in!'
Buffed	When Epic increases a weapon's strength so it causes more damage
Bush campers	Players who hide in bushes
Campers	Players who hide in one spot for as long as possible
Chuggie, chugs	Chug Jug (though some players also use this to refer to slurpies!)
Cracked	Another term for shield pop – when you have successfully destroyed an opponents shield
Crossie	Crossbow
Double pumping	Placing two pump action shotguns in adjoining positions in your inventory so you can get two shots off quickly
Half-pod	A potion that will give you 50% shield
Heals	Any item that increases armour or health. 'You got any heals' means someone is asking if you have any items that can help them be tougher to eliminate.

WHAT THEY SAY	WHAT THEY MEAN
Hot drop	Landing in a location popular with lots of other players is known as performing a hot drop
Knocked	Taking an enemy down without killing them in squads or duos
Legendary SCAR	Epic or Legendary Assault Rifle
Loot bait	The practice of leaving lots of loot on display, then hiding nearby and waiting for someone to come and try to collect it all
Low ground warrior	A player that can't build very well so they build only small structures or very low ones
Mats	Short for materials – the things you use to build structures in the game
Meds	Any item that increases your health – but not your shield
Minis	Mini shield
Nerfed	A weapon or location that has been made much weaker so it is virtually useless. The opposite of buffed.
Nineties/busting nineties	A way of building towers using ramps that constantly turn through 90 degrees
N00b/Noob	Someone who is new to the game – and usually not playing it very well, by making basic mistakes
No scope	The art of eliminating someone using a sniper rifle without looking down the scope first
No-skin	This refers to players using the default outfits. It CAN signal a new player, but often advanced players use no-skins to trick opponents into thinking they are new players.
NPC	Non-playble character. These are the characters around the map you can interact with, buy goods from or hire to help you.
OG	Original Gangster. Someone who has played the game since the very early days, normally identified by their use of older skins that show how experienced they are.
OP	Overpowered. This means a weapon or vehicle is just too strong, giving players an unfair advantage.
Ping	This has two meanings. It can mean you have marked the location of an enemy of weapon on the map to your team-mates. Alternatively, it can describe the speed of your internet connection. Higher ping means a poorer connection and more lag.
POI	Points of Interest on the map – landmarks you can visit that are usually home to some goodies
Res	Resuscitate – if a team mate calls 'res me' it means they need you to revive them quickly!
Shield pop	Destroying an opponent's shield, leaving them vulnerable to further damage
Slurpie	Slurp Juice
Storm Troopers	Players who hide in the storm to avoid opponents shooting them
Sweat	A sweat is a player trying so hard to win that they have probably broken into a sweat
Supped	Suppressed – so a 'supped pistol' is a supressed pistol
Taccie	Tactical Shotgun
Tagged	To hit an opponent with one or two shots but not take them down completely
Turtling	Building a 1x1 cube with a roof on to heal inside, or to use to snipe from
Vaulted	Weapons that have been removed from the game for the time being

QUIZ CORNER!

THINK YOU'RE A FORTNITE SUPERFAN? THEN TRY OUT OUR AWESOME QUIZ – AT THE ANSWERS ARE OVERLEAF. BUT NO PEEKING AT THE ANSWERS – THAT'S NOT THE FORTNITE WAY! THINKING CAPS ON, PENCILS OUT, AND LET'S GET QUIZZICAL!

1 WHAT TYPE OF ANIMAL PINATA WILL YOU FIND WEAPONS INSIDE OF IN FORTNITE?
a) Llama
b) Donkey
c) Sheep
d) Chicken

2 WHAT WAS THE NAME OF THE EQUIPMENT MIDAS USED TO TRY AND CONTROL THE STORM?
a) The contraption
b) The thing
c) The device
d) The whatsit

3 WHAT DOES IT MEAN WHEN A WEAPON HAS BEEN 'NERFED'?
a) It has been made stronger
b) It has been made weaker
c) It is no longer available
d) It only fires foam bullets now

4 WHAT CREATURE ATE MIDAS AT THE END OF CHAPTER 2 SEASON 2?
a) A crocodile
b) A dinosaur
c) A lion
d) A shark

5 WHICH IS NOT A CATEGORY OF FORTNITE WEAPON?
a) Rare
b) Legendary
c) Awesome
d) Uncommon

SOLO
CHANGE
PLAY!

76

9 AT THE END OF WHICH SEASON DID TONY STARK LEAD A FLEET OF BATTLE BUSSES AGAINST GALACTUS?

a) Chapter 2 Season 1
b) Chapter 2 Season 2
c) Chapter 2 Season 4
d) Chapter 2 Season 6

6 WHICH OF THESE FILM FRANCHISES HAS NOT HAD A FORTNITE TIE-IN?

a) Avengers
b) Star Wars
c) Alien
d) Mission: Impossible

10 IN FORTNITE, WHO OR WHAT IS FENNIX?

a) A weapon
b) A location
c) An emote
d) A skin

7 WHICH VEHICLE HASN'T EVER BEEN AVAILABLE IN FORTNITE?

a) Cars
b) Choppers
c) Motorbikes
d) Motorboats

11 WHICH MUSICIAN GAVE FORTNITE'S FIRST EVER GIG?

a) Dua Lipa
b) Marshmello
c) Kanye West
d) Travis Scott

8 HOW MANY INVENTORY SLOTS DO YOU HAVE IN FORTNITE?

a) 4
b) 5
c) 6
d) 7

12 WHAT COLOUR IS AN EPIC WEAPON IN YOUR INVENTORY

a) Red
b) Blue
c) Green
d) Purple

QUIZ ANSWERS!

IT'S THE MOMENT OF TRUTH! HOW DID YOU GET ON WITH OUR FIENDISH FORTNITE TEST?

THE ANSWERS ARE BELOW!

1	a	5	c	9	c
2	c	6	d	10	d
3	b	7	c	11	b
4	d	8	b	12	d

snk eliminated _____ISOWFIFE97 with a rifle

5000   186

30 / 218 ASSAULT RIFLE   6 248   243   32

100
100

HOW DID YOU SCORE?

0-3 COMMON

Have you even read this Annual? You're the kind of Fortnite gamer that rarely gets to see the second storm circle aren't you? You definitely need to spend some time learning the basics but don't worry you'll get there – with a little help!

4-6 RARE

You're getting there, but there's still a lot of work to do! Learn your landing sites in a little more detail, master your loadout and gather more materials early in the game and you'll be making it into the later stages of Battle Royalés. Keep this book by your bedside and you'll have the hang of it all in no time!

7-9 EPIC

Now we're talking! You'll regularly find yourself making it into the top 25; we just need to work on your pro skills a little bit to turn that into top tens! With just a little bit more practice and attention, you could soon find yourself even higher up that leaderboard!

10-12: LEGENDARY

Ok, we got a bad ass in the house! You're a regular top ten finisher, and a frequent wniner of Victory Royales. Hone this skills, suit up in your favourite skin, grab your best back bling from the locker, and lets head straight to the battle bus!